RECOGNIZING
THE OPPORTUNITY

■

WEALTH MANAGEMENT,
ESTATE PLANNING & LIFE INSURANCE

Recognizing the Opportunity: Wealth Management, Estate Planning and Life Insurance
By Russ Alan Prince, Hannah Shaw Grove, Brett Van Bortel & Richard L. Harris

Charter Financial Publishing Network
499 Broad Street, Suite 120
Shrewsbury, NJ 07702
Tel: 732.450.8866
Fax: 732.450.8877
www.pw-mag.com

Disclaimer
This book is designed to provide accurate and authoritative information on the subject matter covered. This publication is sold with the understanding that neither the publisher nor the authors are engaged in rendering legal, medical, accounting, financial or other professional service or advice in specific situations. Although prepared by professionals, this publication should not be utilized as a substitute for professional advice in specific situations. If legal, medical, accounting, financial or other professional advice is required the services of the appropriate professional should be sought. Neither the authors nor the publisher may be held liable for any misuse or misinterpretation of the information in this publication. All information provided is believed and intended to be reliable, but accuracy cannot be guaranteed by the authors or the publisher.

ISBN: 978-0-9766574-4-6

To Luigi (of the Flying Luigis) and the Lady who saved him
– Russ

For constancy and adventure, to my parents
– Hannah

To my family, and the simple pleasures
and great treasures of our life together
– Brett

To the real treasures—my family
– Richard

TABLE OF CONTENTS

ABOUT THIS BOOK

We regularly conduct group training sessions and one-on-one coaching for advisors who are interested in becoming wealth managers. The common goal of the professionals we work with is a desire to expand their offerings to affluent clients and, in the process, make themselves a more valuable resource. There are a number of obstacles a financial advisor faces when migrating to a wealth management platform, but among the most consistently difficult is the understanding and implementation of the advanced planning process and its results. One of the debilitating obstacles proves to be the use of life insurance in estate planning strategies. Many financial advisors are not technically proficient in life insurance, nor do they understand how it fits in a client's portfolio or how it can be leveraged and structured to accomplish estate planning goals.

Of equal importance is the role estate planning and life insurance can play in building an advisor's business. Together, estate planning and life insurance enable a financial advisor to learn more about affluent clients and their goals, become more involved in the delivery of client solutions, and cultivate long-term, trusting relationships with their clients. The bonus, however, is that life insurance can be an exceptionally lucrative product and, as such, it can play an important role in the growth of an advisor's revenue and personal income.

Who Can Benefit?

In working with a variety of advisors—especially investment professionals—we quickly realized that a primer on the relationship between wealth management, estate planning, and life insurance would be a useful addition to any advisor's library.

This book is for any wealth manager—whether you are new to the business or a seasoned practitioner—who wants to do a better job understanding and meeting the needs of your affluent clients and become more successful in the process. More specifically, this book and the data, insights and processes detailed within will help:

- wealth managers who want to be more effective introducing estate planning and life insurance solutions to their wealthy clients;
- any type of advisor (including investment advisors, private bankers, accountants, and brokers) in the process of transitioning to a wealth management platform;
- P&C brokers hoping to expand their business with the introduction of additional insurance-related products and services;
- any financial professional who wants to offer life insurance as part of their suite of products and services.

By contrast, this book is *not* for life insurance specialists or any professional with an expertise in the use of life insurance in the estate planning process. It is written for wealth managers (and financial advisors who are transitioning to wealth management) who are comfortable working with a network of third-party experts to deliver the specialized skills and products required in the wealth management process—and want to improve their ability to recognize opportunities to do so.

What Can You Expect?

This book was developed with the intent of providing an overview of wealth management and the various roles and applications of life insurance within the discipline in conceptual terms and through the use of a relatively few highly simplified blind examples. And, most importantly, provide insights on how to consistently identify the opportunities to deliver life insurance as part of a client's wealth management experience.

As expected, we begin with the basics. In the first two sections of the book we size the prospective universe of affluent clients, those individuals for whom wealth management and estate planning is both desired and needed, and we provide a status on the ever-changing and heavily debated estate tax. We follow those fundamentals with a detailed discussion of wealth management and its appeal to practitioners and wealthy clients, and we include information on the factors that habitually result in poor estate plans or estate plans that are never implemented. Next we share a proven process for developing an in-depth understanding of clients—the Whole Client Model. This process is central to all successful wealth management practices and the basis for identifying estate planning and life insurance opportunities within your book of business.

The third and final section of the book is dedicated to the role of life insurance in estate planning. We examine in detail the uses of life insurance and the various funding strategies, and provide blind case studies to illustrate how each of the strategies and techniques work in real client situations.

While this book contains a wealth of information on the wealth management process and the intricacies of the underlying products and services specific to estate planning, there are limitations to the format, and no book will ever replace hands-on experience and the practical application of concepts. We do, however, know that by studying the primer you will develop a greater familiarity with the topic and a greater sensitivity to the areas in which you can deliver more value to your wealthy clients. Good luck!

PART I

■

THE WEALTHY AND ESTATE PLANNING

CHAPTER 1

■

THE WORLD OF EXCEPTIONAL WEALTH

The high-net-worth occupy a desirable social standing in today's society. As a result, they are lionized for their accomplishments and their assets and scrutinized for their idiosyncrasies and behavior. Without question, the pursuit of wealth is one of mankind's great obsessions. Achieving millionaire status is commonly cited as the "American Dream" and now it is a dream that is attainable for more people than ever before.

As a group and as individuals, the affluent are recognized and defined by their level of wealth—which today totals $61.7 trillion in aggregate. The affluent can be further understood by the interplay of five core characteristics in conjunction with their high-net-worth personalities. In this chapter we will provide analytically derived estimates on the size of the potential universe of estate planning clients, and insights on their financial mindset and motivations.

The Size of the Market for Estate Planning

We often hear advisors lamenting the lack of wealthy clients and prospects. It's a pervasive complaint, but an unfounded one. Based on our analysis, there has never been a time nor place with as many rich people as the United States has today. Despite some financial reversals over the past few years (a volatile stock market and declining real estate market, for example), the overall appreciation of assets coupled with an economic and social environment that strongly rewards entrepreneurs has created a boom in private wealth. Consequently, there has been an increase in wealthy individuals, a need for those wealthy individuals to protect and manage their sizeable estates, and an opportunity to use life insurance in the implementation of estate plans.

The reality is that there are more than enough "rich people" but the tricky part is finding them and securing their business. We are frequently asked to help advisors understand and master the most effective methods of creating a pipeline of new, affluent clients. While these methodologies and techniques are not the focus of *Recognizing the Opportunity*, it is worth noting that wealth managers are more capable than investment generalists and product specialists of forging the professional relationships and cultivating the client satisfaction that can yield a steady stream of qualified, wealthy individuals that are receptive to financial advice and products. And part of being a wealth manager is expanding your repertoire to include a broad array of the products and services a wealthy client might need, including life insurance.

To calculate the size of the affluent market and, in turn, the size of the business opportunity, we developed an analytical model that revealed some favorable trends. The universe of private wealth is large and growing, which can have a direct influence on building a successful wealth management business.

The model used as its foundation previous analytic models we developed for similar purposes. Those models were updated, taking into account the actual and perceived differential of selected assets including business interests, real property, and collectibles. Furthermore, and of critical importance to the current model, we took into account the impact of the "underground economy" in the United States on private wealth creation, limiting our analysis to "tax avoision" and related activities. Any wealth created through illegal activities, such as drug dealing or money laundering, was excluded from the model. It is important to note that the model's projections include the high-net-worth that are subject to US taxes, including estate tax, and is not restricted to United States citizens, United States residents, nor individuals with a primarily domicile in the United States.

We then leveraged the model's output to size the universe of individuals and/ or families with a net worth of $10 million or more. While it is not mandatory for a client to have an estate valued at $10 million in order to benefit from estate planning and the associated life insurance solutions, larger estates increase the likelihood that the strategies discussed in this book will be viable. Conversely, many clients with estates smaller than $10 million can benefit from life insurance and should not be overlooked. The following chart includes a best case, worst case and most likely determination for the number of affluent families (Exhibit 1.1).

EXHIBIT 1.1
The Number of Affluent

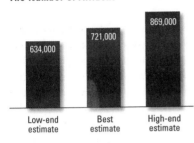

The following chart displays the aggregate wealth controlled by these affluent families. For methodological purposes, the amount of private wealth per affluent family was capped at $2.6 billion. Once again, we considered a best case, worst case and most likely calculation (Exhibit 1.2).

Without a wealth tax that some countries impose, it is impossible to know the exact size and scope of private wealth in the U.S. and even with the use of statistical modeling techniques there is a margin of error. Nevertheless, the model's output indicates a great many affluent families controlling enormous wealth. That fact, coupled with the very likely persistence of estate taxes *(see Chapter 2: The State of Estate Planning)*, strongly supports the feasibility of providing life insurance now and in the future.

The remainder of this chapter is devoted to discussing critical macro-perspectives of the affluent.

EXHIBIT 1.2
Aggregate Wealth Controlled by the Affluent

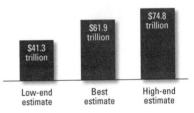

Core Characteristics of the Affluent

As noted previously, the affluent are principally distinguished by their wealth. Our extensive research and hands-on work with the high-net-worth shows that they have other common traits—five core characteristics that relate to the way they think about and use their wealth. The five core characteristics of the affluent are:

■ **Complexity.** The personal and financial lives of the affluent tend to be more complicated. External factors, such as tax and estate laws, naturally play a far larger role in their lives than they do for the less wealthy, and the affluent are often constrained when it comes to their capital. Another area of intense complexity for the affluent is created by their family dynamics and money often magnifies eccentricities, idiosyncrasies, and animosities.

■ **Control.** Money and power walk hand-in-hand, so it is no surprise that the affluent are often focused on ensuring appropriate levels of control. A great many want to exercise a measure of control or influence over just about every situation of significance in their lives. In the end, control is demonstrated by the way the wealth is structured in the estate plan.

■ **Connections.** Success is often not exclusively measured by money. The Chinese have a word for it, and that word is guanxi—connections. It's sometimes said that with the right guanxi, the right connections, almost anything is possible. Among the affluent, the judicious use of their contacts can facilitate personal and business success. These relationships are highly prized and are therefore well protected.

■ **Capital.** By capital, we do not mean wealth per se, but the way that the affluent use money to define themselves. Capital, in this context, is the ability to deploy resources to make things happen that is, not money itself, but what money can accomplish.

■ **Charity.** Based on our research, we have found that, for the most part, the affluent are not charitable simply because of the tax incentives and the desire to see their name chiseled in stone as benefactors; they are earnestly looking for ways to "make the world a better place." And, with their wealth established, charity often becomes an important consideration.

Of course, beyond these core characteristics, the affluent are as distinct and diverse as any group of individuals. It's your job—as a wealth manager—to understand both the general and specific details of each of your affluent clients, to be fully attuned to their similarities as well as their distinctions which is where a comprehensive profiling methodology is so important *(see Chapter 5: The Whole Client Model).*

The High-Net-Worth Personalities

The affluent, as seen through the prism of their five core characteristics, is a distinct market segment. Nevertheless, when it comes to money, there are nine different high-net-worth personalities. By understanding the nine high-net-worth personalities, you're better able to understand and communicate with your affluent clients and this translates into stronger and more productive relationships.

The creation of psychographic segments—or personalities—involved using the multidimensional statistical tools of factor and cluster analysis on the body of data collected from the affluent about sophisticated services and related financial products (i.e., estate planning and life insurance). The following provides an overview of the nine high-net-worth personalities and some of their key attributes:

■ **Family Stewards** are motivated by the need to protect their families over the long-term. They're highly concerned for the safety of their families and they are highly motivated to take action to protect them now and in the future.

■ **Phobics** dislike thinking about money. Moreover, they do not want to be directly involved in managing their financial affairs, which necessitates depending heavily on a primary advisor for assistance.

■ **Independents** see attention to financial issues as a necessary evil. Their primary objective in accumulating assets is to achieve financial independence and the accompanying security it brings.

■ **The Anonymous** have a deep-seated—and sometimes irrational—need for privacy and confidentiality in all financial and personal dealings.

■ **Moguls** are motivated to accumulate more assets in order to achieve personal power and, by extension, influence. In short, they want to leverage the power conferred by wealth.

■ **VIPs** are motivated to accumulate assets and utilize their wealth, in part, to achieve greater status and prestige. This personality prizes the favorable opinion of select others above all else.

■ **Accumulators** strive to build their personal assets out of an overriding concern for personal financial well-being. The "collecting of wealth" is a bulwark against an uncertain future.

■ **Gamblers** view financial affairs as a personal challenge, but one that they are very capable of handling. They believe their skills and competence will protect them from all significant financial threats, and are actively involved in the management of their finances.

■ **Innovators** believe their analytical capabilities will sustain them and protect them from external threats. And, because of their life-long use of their analytic capabilities, they are highly self-reliant and do not delegate any portion of life tasks having to do with analysis.

The High-Net-Worth Personalities and Core Characteristics

A meta-framework overlapping the five core characteristics of the affluent and the high-net-worth personality model provides insights useful in working with the wealthy (Exhibit 1.3). As shown, each high-net-worth personality has different complexity, control, connections, capital, and charitable attributes and needs.

More information on the characteristics and motivations of each high-net-worth personality and the methods that can be used to profile wealthy clients can be found in *Appendix A: High-Net-Worth Psychology*.

Implications

By any measure, 721,000 wealthy families with an aggregate net worth of $61.9 trillion represents a large opportunity for adroit and focused financial advisors who offer a wealth management platform. Given the size, and likely complexity,

EXHIBIT 1.3

The Interplay of the Core Characteristics and the High-Net-Worth Personalities

HNW PERSONALITIES	COMPLEXITY	CONTROL	CONNECTIONS	CAPITAL	CHARITY
Family Stewards	Family political dynamics significant	Current controlling generation resists succession	Principal connections are family ties – easiest to leverage horizontally	Need to maintain family control over the business	Desire to make a better world for their children and communicate critical values to them
Phobics	Difficult to manage information flow with this segment	Seeking to replace control with trust	Well-qualified social network of peers	Highly oriented towards conservation of capital	Want results without personally attending to financial and legal details.
Independents	Complex because not always available for decision-making	Seek control over personal activities and autonomy	Prefers few good friends and business associates to many acquaintances	Conservation of capital needs outweigh interest in investments	Tied to instruments that help them assure their goal of personal financial independence
Anonymous	Difficult to manage because of security concerns	Need highest control over privacy and confidentality	Network limited but tight	Privacy needs drive investment decision-making	Seek to preserve anonymity in giving
Moguls	Will tolerate complexity in planning and management	Highest control needs of all the segments	Network focused downward so power can be exerted	Highly oriented towards new investments (more control opportunities)	Another avenue they can use to exert power and influence
VIPs	Need for public recognition creates complexity	Need control over personal image and reputation	Network focused upward, in direction of aspiration; social ties shallower	Will invest in vehicles that create public image	Another avenue for status, prestige and recognition
Accumulators	Vast and diverse holdings create complex situations	Demand high levels of control and frequent reporting	Medium network; heterogeneous in character	Will accept investment if capital conservation objectives met	Not highly charitably oriented
Gamblers	Complexity created by need for intense	Seeking a wide variety of opportunities, not control	Moderate network characterized by intense	Most risk-tolerant of all segments, highly	Often directly connected to financial returns

of the estates in question it is probably fair to say that talented and capable estate planners and life insurance providers will benefit as well.

To capitalize on this opportunity, you must understand the wealthy at both strategic and tactical levels. Familiarity with the five core characteristics and the nine high-net-worth personalities provides a proven strategic perspective and a philosophy on which your approach to customer interaction can be based. While, this strategic perspective provides a broad, conceptual understanding of the affluent, you will still need to spend time getting to know individual clients well in order to work with them in a customized and consultative way. One of the most effective processes for accomplishing this is the profiling technique discussed in a later chapter *(see Chapter 5: The Whole Client Model)*.

CHAPTER 2

■

THE STATE
OF ESTATE PLANNING

Most estate planning professionals are concerned that the business of estate planning, and logically the provision of life insurance in conjunction with estate planning, might vanish. Admittedly, there is a movement afoot to abolish the estate tax, driven by and supported in large part by the very wealthy for obvious reasons. However, all indications are that the estate tax—in some form or another—will be around for some time to come. This fact, along with issues surrounding business succession, the need for estate equalization, and the desire to control the distribution and use of their wealth from the grave means that life insurance will continue to offer attractive benefits to the wealthy.

These things in combination with the status of most estate plans creates an enormous opportunity for advisors who can consult on estate planning issues and work with other experts to provide life insurance based solutions.

Before proceeding, a common understanding of estate planning is paramount. For the purposes of this book, we define it as follows:

Estate planning is the process of legally structuring the
future disposition of current and projected assets.

As noted in *Chapter 1: The World of Exceptional Wealth*, the affluent have a fondness for control and estate planning is one way they can actualize this desire. To be sure, estate planning is a process that can help mitigate estate taxes, and the ability to limit what goes to the Treasury's coffers can be a wonderful motivation. But this result is often a nice byproduct of a process that was initiated for personal and emotional reasons. In fact, a meaningful part of estate planning for the affluent is being able to dictate to whom and under what conditions their assets will go when they die.

■ **Mac, a successful business owner, wants to make sure the company is transferred to his son, Henry,** *who has been involved in the business since his early teens. Mac believes that Henry is prepared to run the business and is the most capable of his relatives. He also wants to avoid an intra-family struggle for control that would take the focus off the business during a critical time. As a result, he will need the appropriate plan in place to ensure the desired succession, along with a way to provide equally for Henry's siblings.*

■ **Ginnie and Mark have been married for 30 years and place significant value on fiscal responsibility and education.** *They also recognize that their three children—Bettina (26), Josephine (24) and Mark Jr. (21)—have grown up without financial limitations and are not mature enough to take control of their inheritance. They want a plan that will outline explicit restrictions and name a trustee to monitor spending and provide guidance.*

■ **Fatima just divorced her second husband and secured an eight-figure settlement.** *She wants to provide generously for her 10-year old twins, Marina and Oscar, while protecting her assets from her ex-husband's new wife and children.*

These, and countless other examples, call for rigorous and thoughtful estate planning whether or not there are estate taxes to contend with, especially for people with significant assets and complex familial relationships

Public Opinion Favors Estate Taxes

The elimination of federal estate taxes could dramatically change the nature of most estate planning activities. But federal estate taxes are unlikely to be repealed permanently due in large part to budgetary concerns at the federal and state level, and the surprising support of the super-rich.

Approximately 50,000 estates pay estate taxes in the U.S. each year and this equals roughly $30 billion dollars in revenue. Given the increase in private wealth over the last decade, estate taxes will likely become an even greater source of governmental revenue moving forward. Under the current law, the federal estate tax will be temporarily phased out and eventually reinstated in full force. In 2002, 38 states began losing some of the revenue they previously received through their state pick-up tax. To bridge the gap, many states have imposed their own estate taxes and benefited from the revenue cushion. Regardless of the outcome on the federal estate tax, it is foolish to assume the states will readily rescind their own estate taxes without prompting.

While most of the public—including the very wealthy—is against permanent repeal, it is probable that both federal and state level estate taxes will be modified numerous times. It is also possible that estate taxes will be increased in an effort to offset other tax decreases that could strengthen the economy with business and job growth. Both scenarios mean estate planning will continue to be a necessity for the affluent.

The Wealthy Favor Estate Taxes

One of the most visible and vocal supporters of the estate tax has been Warren Buffett. Interestingly, our research reveals that this attitude is not unique to the uber-wealthy. In a survey of 298 individuals, each with a net worth of $5 million or more, 84.6% are against a complete repeal of the Federal estate tax. At the same time, 78.9% are in favor of modifying the Federal estate tax to some extent (Exhibit 2.1).

EXHIBIT 2.1
Public Opposition to Estate Tax Elimination

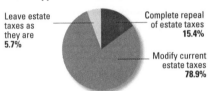

Leave estate taxes as they are **5.7%**

Complete repeal of estate taxes **15.4%**

Modify current estate taxes **78.9%**

N = 298 individuals with estates of $5 million or more

And while the majority of millionaires surveyed feel that the estate tax in its current form is unfair, almost half of individuals surveyed believe that the wealthy should bear a larger share of the tax burden and nearly all believe that reform and/or reduction of the estate tax would be sound fiscal policy (Exhibit 2.2).

EXHIBIT 2.2
What the Wealthy Think About the Federal Estate Tax

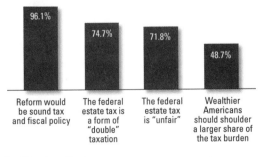

96.1%	74.7%	71.8%	48.7%
Reform would be sound tax and fiscal policy	The federal estate tax is a form of "double" taxation	The federal estate tax is "unfair"	Wealthier Americans should shoulder a larger share of the tax burden

N = 483 American millionaires

Another death tax that should be considered comes from the state, although it is often overlooked as the high-net-worth and their estate planning professionals focus their efforts on minimizing the impact of the Federal assessment. This oversight can result in complications during the estate settlement process, as well as additional costs in the form of taxes and penalties. *See Appendix C: The Implications of State Death Taxes* for more information.

The Estate Planning Opportunity

According to our research, most wealthy individuals already have estate plans (for the purposes of research, an estate plan was defined as something more than a will) but financial advisors should not let this fact discourage them. In a study with 563 individuals with estates of $10 million or more, only 10.3% did not have an estate plan.

Collectively, the use of estate plans is strong but there are some minor distinctions by source of wealth that are worth noting (Exhibit 2.3). Individuals with inherited wealth were the most likely to have an estate plan (in addition to the trusts and other legal structures established for them) with 97.8% responding in the affirmative. Corporate executives were the second largest group with estate plans at 95.9%. All kinds of business owners were still represented in the majority, but at slightly lower levels than that of other affluent respondents, with 88.7% of business owners and 82.9% of family business owners (transferring the business to an immediate family member or relative) having plans.

EXHIBIT 2.3
The Affluent Have Estate Planning

	CORPORATE EXECUTIVES	BUSINESS OWNERS	FAMILY BUSINESS OWNERS	INHERITORS	WEIGHTED AVERAGE
Have an Estate Plan	95.9%	88.7%	82.9%	97.8%	89.7%
Do Not Have an Estate Plan	4.1%	11.3%	17.1%	2.2%	10.3%
Sample Size	122	159	193	89	563

The high acceptance of estate plans among the wealthy is a positive sign that demonstrates a recognition of the need and a willingness to participate in the process. This means an advisor can broach an estate planning conversation knowing that his clients are informed and receptive.

Unfortunately, there are a variety of reasons that prevent estate plans from being implemented. In these cases, a wealthy individual risks losing control of the manner in which their assets will be distributed and may subject their estates and heirs to unnecessary taxation. *See Appendix B: The Implementation Obstacles of Estate*

Planning for more information.

For an estate plan to be effective, it must be up-to-date and reflective of the client's personal and professional circumstances and their plans for their assets. Unfortunately, most clients approach the estate planning process as a one-time event and have never gone back to review or amend the original plan after it was approved. To get a better feel for the frequency with which a plan should be reviewed, we asked 202 private client lawyers for their opinion (Exhibit 2.4). Nearly three-quarters of attorneys say a plan is stale after just two years.

Using the guidelines specified by attorneys, more than 90% of the afflu-ent have out-of-date estate plans (Exhibit 2.5). These plans become outdated for many reasons from the wealthy person becoming wealthier to a significant

EXHIBIT 2.4
When an Estate Plan is "Stale"

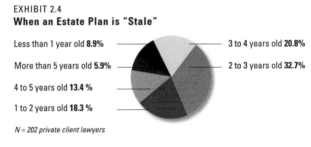

Less than 1 year old **8.9%**

More than 5 years old **5.9%**

4 to 5 years old **13.4 %**

1 to 2 years old **18.3 %**

3 to 4 years old **20.8%**

2 to 3 years old **32.7%**

N = 202 private client lawyers

EXHIBIT 2.5
The Age of Affluent Estate Plans

	CORPORATE EXECUTIVES	BUSINESS OWNERS	FAMILY BUSINESS OWNERS	INHERITORS	WEIGHTED AVERAGE
Less than 4 years old	10.3%	5.7%	4.4%	20.7%	8.9%
4 or more years old	89.7%	94.3%	95.6%	79.3%	91.1%
Sample Size	117	141	160	89	505

change in circumstances such as marriage or divorce. The issue is most pro-nounced in the two types of business owners, but all wealthy individuals should update their plans more regularly and would benefit from the involvement and oversight of a wealth manager.

Implications

Estate planning is important as long as there is an estate tax, but the interest in and need for estate planning among the wealthy extends far beyond tax mitigation. The wealthy have embraced the benefits of estate planning as a means of managing their tax burden and controlling the distribution of their assets, and most high-net-worth individuals have completed at least one version of an estate plan. The majority of private client attorneys feel that most estate plans are woefully outdated and, as such, many wealthy individuals need assistance from professionals to stay abreast of personal and regulatory changes.

Despite its controversial nature, permanent elimination of the federal estate tax is unlikely and will probably be reformed and modified numerous times over the coming decades. These continual changes are another incentive for affluent families to rely on a wealth manager with a comprehensive understanding of their financial situation.

PART II

■

WEALTH MANAGEMENT

CHAPTER 3

■

THE WEALTH
MANAGEMENT MODEL

There is an abundance of scientific evidence supporting the role of wealth managers in the lives and financial affairs of wealthy individuals; we conducted a significant piece of research on the subject that is discussed in detail in *Wealth Management: The New Business Model for Financial Advisors* (Penton Media, 2005 and 2003). Anecdotally speaking, wealth managers can be the single point-of-contact for the broad range of products and services the affluent need. The extent of the services delivered allows the wealth manager to become more involved in the client's life and, therefore, more knowledgeable about the client's circumstances, potential problems, and objectives. This heightened awareness can lead to a more consultative and responsive relationship between the client and the wealth manager, which, in turn, leads to higher-quality interactions and higher client satisfaction. Ultimately, these enhancements can lead to the wealth manager assuming a more prominent role, having access to a greater portion of the client's portfolio and more business opportunities. In short, wealth management can result in multiple benefits for both the clients and the wealth managers themselves.

Given this scenario, it's no surprise to learn that a large number of financial advisors call themselves "wealth managers." Unfortunately, our research indicates that many professionals use the title without the credentials or the capability to deliver a wealth management experience to their clients. In a survey of 512 advisors that derived 85% or more of their revenue from investment products, 77.9% refer to themselves as wealth managers (Exhibit 3.1). This means that very rarely, if ever,

EXHIBIT 3.1
Call Themselves Wealth Managers

Self-described
wealth managers
77.9%

N = 512 Financial Advisors
Source: Cultivating the Middle-class Millionaire:
Why Financial Advisors are Failing their Wealthy
Clients and What They Can Do About It (Wealth
Management Press, *2005)*

do these advisors deliver a non-investment related solution to their clients.

In reality, very few advice practitioners are wealth managers. The in-name-only wealth managers changed their title (and most likely their office signage, business cards and stationery) but made few or no changes to their practices. In fact, when we conducted research with financial advisors to understand their practices, the scope of their relationships with their high-net-worth clients, and the sources of their revenue and income, fewer than 10% of surveyed advisors have businesses that met the definition of wealth management—and therein lies an important obstacle to success.

Wealth Management Defined

During our training and coaching work with advisors, we regularly ask for their thoughts about and definitions of wealth management. In addition to the expected handful of obscure answers, most advisors equate wealth management with investment management, more specifically tax-efficient investment management. This is a predictable outcome, since our research cited above reveals that most "wealth managers" have built their business around investment products. Alone, however, investment products cannot deliver the comprehensive solutions that wealth management clients need and expect.

Since wealth management is a process that entails two parties, we believe that the definition should include both perspectives:

■ An exceptionally affluent client experiences wealth management as the ongoing solution of their financial problems or the overall enhancement of their financial situation.

■ The wealth manager resolves a client's financial needs and wants with the thoughtful use of various financial products, often requiring partnership with other experts and specialists.

In other words, wealth management is *solving affluent clients' financial solutions by delivering of a broad range of financial products and services in a highly consultative way* that reflects the client's unique profile.

By broadening the range of products used, wealth management can help mitigate the impact poor investment performance can have on the relationship between advisors and their clients while providing opportunities to strengthen the relationship in other ways.

The Rewards of Wealth Management

Wealth management is not just about breadth of product, but also about depth of information and resources. If your expertise is in investment management, to be a successful wealth manager, you must be willing to step outside the footprint of your current business and expand your capabilities. It's a complicated and sometimes frustrating process, but done properly, can deliver impressive results. Satisfaction is much higher among the clients of wealth managers, and practitioners of wealth management report a much higher average income than their counterparts who offer a more restricted range of financial products.

In a study of 1,281 advisors, the average wealth manager generates more than twice as much in gross production than the average investment advisor and has about ten times as many assets under management. Yet the wealth manager has only a fraction of the clients to deal with. For the majority of financial advisors, wealth management is a more profitable and efficient practice model than investment management by itself (Exhibit 3.2).

This phenomenon can be observed in other businesses as well. We surveyed 98

EXHIBIT 3.2
Comparing Practice Models

FACTORS	INVESTMENT ADVISORS	WEALTH MANAGERS
Average gross production	$670,000	$1,360,000
Average assets under management	$31 million	$301 million
Average number of clients	220	70

N = 1,281 financial advisors

private banks where the minimum account size was $500,000 in investable assets and empirically identified three service models:

■ **Basic.** These private banks provided traditional banking services augmented with investment management and trust services.

■ **Enhanced.** These private banks offered the Basic model and credit.

■ **Wealth Management.** These private banks offered the Enhanced model along with a variety of advanced legal planning services, such as estate planning and asset protection planning, and the products needed to implement the plans.

About half of the private banks (46.9%) offered their clients the Basic service model; 29.6% delivered the Enhanced service model; 23.5% offered wealth management (Exhibit 3.3). Using the profitability numbers from the banks in each service model, we built analytic models that allowed us to financially compare the three types. We statistically controlled for variables such as the wealth of the clientele and how long they had been clients of the banks. This methodological approach enables us to compare the private banks in an apples-to-apples manner.

EXHIBIT 3.3
The Service Models of Private Banks

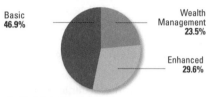

Basic
46.9%

Wealth Management
23.5%

Enhanced
29.6%

N = 98 private banks
Source: Wealth Management: A New Business Model for Financial Advisors *(Wealth Management Press, 2003)*

In order to illustrate the profit variances, we created an index by setting the base profitability of bank segment employing the Basic service model at $1,000. Private banks that had implemented the Enhanced menu of services earned significantly more, or $1,134 on the index. Finally, private banks that employed the Wealth Management service model more than doubled the profitability of the Basic version (Exhibit 3.4). The conclusion is inarguable: the ability to offer affluent clients a broader platform of expertise and products results in greater profitability for private banks.

EXHIBIT 3.4
**The Service Models
and Private Bank Profitability**

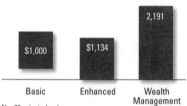

Basic	Enhanced	Wealth Management
$1,000	$1,134	2,191

N = 98 private banks
Source: Wealth Management: A New Business Model for Financial Advisors *(Wealth Management Press, 2003)*

Another way to demonstrate the fiscal advantages of the wealth management model to advisors is to review the results of the investment advisors who have successfully transitioned their practices. Moving from an investment-oriented advisory practice to a wealth management practice resulted in an average increase of 35% in first-year income for these practitioners. That means that if you're currently pocketing $200,000 a year as an investment advisor, by making the switch you would take home at least $270,000 in the first year as a wealth manager—and may see continued income growth as you refine and hone your wealth management skills.

The case for wealth management is indisputable, but the realities of adopting the model can be troublesome and problematic. Because wealth management entails so much more than basic investments or brokerage, one of the hurdles to a smooth transition may be climbing the learning curve on new and different products— and it's worth noting that one of the most important, and frequently used, products among the exceptionally wealthy is life insurance.

Uncertain About Life Insurance

Effective wealth managers regularly provide life insurance to their clients and ensure that it happens seamlessly. This requires practice, patience and, more often than not, a partnership with a life insurance specialist. But why enter a partnership when it's more profitable to eliminate a third-party? In a study of 522 financial advisors, roughly 34% of respondents were opposed to offering life insurance. While the remaining 66% were willing to provide it, they were critical of their ability to do so successfully (Exhibit 3.5).

EXHIBIT 3.5
Financial Advisors' Willingness to Provide Life Insurance

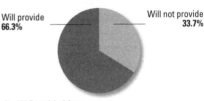

Will provide
66.3%

Will not provide
33.7%

N = 522 financial advisors

Using a factor-analytic approach, six items were identified as the principal reasons that 34% of advisors choose not to sell life insurance (Exhibit 3.6). The reasons make sense for a professional who operates strictly as an investment advisor. But when life insurance is viewed more broadly, as a component of an integrated wealth management process, it can be an effective solution for a variety of needs.

EXHIBIT 3.6
Why Financial Providers Will Not Provide Life Insurance

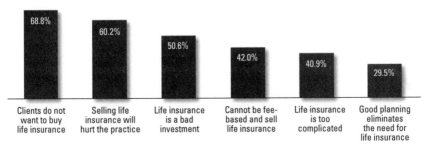

68.8%	60.2%	50.6%	42.0%	40.9%	29.5%
Clients do not want to buy life insurance	Selling life insurance will hurt the practice	Life insurance is a bad investment	Cannot be fee-based and sell life insurance	Life insurance is too complicated	Good planning eliminates the need for life insurance

N = 176 financial advisors

1. The majority of surveyed advisors, 69%, report that clients do not want to buy life insurance and, very often, that is the case. However, affluent clients do want what life insurance can accomplish, such as protection for their families and their businesses and tax-advantaged growth. The critical difference is that wealth managers present life insurance as a tool to achieve the expressed goals of the client (see *Part III: The Role of Life Insurance in Estate Planning*).

2. Another large group of advisors, 60%, feel that selling life insurance would hurt their practices. If a practice is intentionally positioned as an investment-only business, offering life insurance can be confusing to clients. In addition, a poor experience with life insurance can cast a pall on an advisor's reputation. But wealth managers know that managing money cannot solve every financial problem and they keep an open mind when seeking solutions for their clients and forge the professional alliances that will allow them to deliver those solutions.

3. Half of financial advisors cited life insurance as a bad investment and there are usually other vehicles that make more sense. While there are a few instances, such as private placement variable life insurance, in which life insurance is a unique and excellent investment, its principal purpose is not to provide investment results, but rather death benefits which can be deployed at the decedent's direction to pay estates taxes or fund business buy-outs, among other things.

4. Life insurance companies charge premiums for their policies and advisors receive a portion of those premiums in remuneration for selling the product. In fact, wealth managers find that meeting the objectives of their affluent clients usually requires a combination of products that may include commission- and fee-based products. Consequently, a fee-only advisor has made a business decision to focus on a different, and smaller, range of products and will likely not transition their business to a wealth management model.

5. Two-fifths of advisors, or 41%, reported that life insurance is too complicated to add to their menu of offerings. Without question, life insurance is complex and becomes more so when used as part of estate planning. Successful wealth managers know that life insurance is a key element of their wealth management practices and have struck a compromise—they have taken the time to learn the basics, while relying on life insurance specialists to provide the necessary expertise.

6. Almost a third, or 30%, of advisors believe that good estate planning eliminates

the need for insurance. Some estate taxes can, in fact, be eliminated with proper planning. However, taxes on exceptionally large estates may never be completely eliminated. Actuaries will remind us that they make a living analyzing the patterns associated with unexpected events, which means that untimely accidents may compromise a plan that is in progress and not yet complete. Wealth managers do not leave protection to chance and use life insurance to their affluent client's advantage.

There's Still Room for Improvement

The 346 financial advisors in the survey who do provide life insurance are – by their own admission—not very successful at it (Exhibit 3.7). Tellingly, not a single respondent considered themselves "very successful" and only 17% reported being "successful." The remaining 83% categorized themselves as less than successful which means there is considerable room for improvement for these practitioners.

The two issues impacting the effectiveness of these advisors were identified using a factor-analytic methodology – client receptiveness and complexity of the product (Exhibit 3.8). Like the group of advisors who do not offer life insurance, the largest survey sample, 86%, believe that their affluent clients do not want to buy life insurance. And a similarly large number, 73%, find life insurance too difficult to fully understand and represent to their clients.

Again, wealth managers know that specific estate planning strategies require life insurance and often, with the right knowledge, it can be cost-effectively structured. In these types of scenarios, affluent clients are amenable to life insurance because it is presented as a means to an end—the way to meet their goals and objectives.

EXHIBIT 3.7
Success in Providing Life Insurance

N = 346 financial advisors

EXHIBIT 3.8
Obstacles to Providing Life Insurance

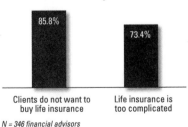

N = 346 financial advisors

As for the complexity of life insurance, there is no question that the nuts-and-bolts of providing the right policies under optimal conditions can be both intricate and difficult. It is for this reason that the framework of the wealth management model is a network of specialists who provide supplemental and complementary talents and expertise. Consequently, two priorities emerge for advisors who want to become wealth managers—the first is the ability to quickly recognize the client situations that will benefit from life insurance and the second is finding a life insurance authority that can be relied upon to deliver accordingly.

The Marketing Mindset

Nicholas is a very successful investment advisor. *He is comfortable and adept at telling his story—how he works, his investment process, his background and credentials, his day-to-day responsibilities and so forth. His approach works very well as an investment advisor. However, in order to generate more business profits, Nicholas decided to become a wealth manager. The same approach to courting clients has proven to be a disaster for him in his new role. And he is not alone in this experience. In fact, the majority of transitioning advisors have had similar results.*

In several research studies, we have seen evidence that nearly all types of financial advisors are focused on selling. In a practical sense, they have a sleeve of products and they spend their time trying to convince prospects to buy what they have. Most financial advisors have a canned presentation they use that provides an overview of the products and services they offer. A more sophisticated version of this sales approach is the use of an institutional-style pitch book. Regardless of the medium, this approach is a perfect example of an advisor-centric model. The flip-side of this model is wealth management—a client-centric approach to providing financial solutions. In evaluating your approach think about the following questions:

- Do you have an established presentation or pitch book that you use with every prospect?
- How much do you know about the prospect and his/her needs before developing an overview of your background and services?
- How do you extract pertinent client information and what level of detail is required before you can create an overview document?
- Are you willing to modify your approach to client meetings based on specific knowledge you have about individual clients?
- How much do you know about the way clients process information and how well do your materials reflect that?

The role of the wealth manager is not to simply sell a financial product to a prospect. Instead, a wealth manager's first concern is to develop a comprehensive understanding of the client. Then, to match the right solutions to the client's needs and desires, and to ensure that they receive an exceptional service experience. After that, product and service sales opportunities will abound. Making the transition is clearly a trade-off between short-term results and long-term success.

The same is true when it comes to providing life insurance—the wealth manager must rigorously maintain a marketing approach to managing the relationship and search for partners that operate with similar standards. The best life insurance specialist for a wealth manager is one that will focus on finding opportunities for life insurance rather than selling it whenever possible. Life insurance can often be part of the solution to an assortment of financial and estate planning problems, but it is not always the right answer and that should not be an obstacle for either practitioner.

Implications

Wealth management is an approach that holds great appeal for high-net-worth clients and can help many advisors achieve a new level of success. Many advisors have embraced the title, but have yet to truly transition their practices from their current investment-oriented models. The rewards for advisors who do make the transition are meaningful—including an increase in first-year income of 35% or more and the ability to focus on fewer, larger clients.

Life insurance is one of the financial products that seasoned wealth managers provide to their affluent clients, but many less experienced advisors are intimidated by life insurance or don't believe that their clients want it or will be receptive to it. One way for an advisor to tackle these concerns is by adopting a marketing mindset and working closely with clients to understand their state of affairs, pressing issues and long-term objectives and craft solutions that reflect those very things. Said another way, they don't sell life insurance but rather solve a problem near and dear to the client. Life insurance is only the tool. Other strategies an advisor can use to avoid common mistakes in the implementation of wealth management, estate planning, and life insurance are discussed in the following chapter.

CHAPTER 4

■

CRITICAL
FAILURE FACTORS

Thus far we've established the following:

■ There are a significant number of individuals and families in the US with asset levels that warrant sophisticated wealth management and estate planning services, which could result in the use of life insurance.

■ The most probable outcome for the federal estate tax is reform, not repeal, and state-level estate taxes are expected to remain.

■ The wealthy often have reasons that extend beyond tax management to use estate planning strategies.

■ The exceptionally affluent will continue to need estate planning assistance and the benefits that come from using life insurance solutions.

■ Wealth management is the approach that best facilitates consultative and customized solutions and results in high client satisfaction.

■ Wealth management is the optimum model for an advisor who wants to readily identify new business opportunities and act on them.

These conditions help create an environment that is ripe with opportunity for wealth managers, estate planners, and life insurance specialists. The bottom line, however, is that many advice practitioners miss the opportunities to provide life-insurance based solutions. In a multi-year program deconstructing and analyzing advisors' businesses we identified the three biggest contributors to this common oversight. They are:

- **Critical Failure Factor #1: Lack of Client Knowledge.** Advisors fail to uncover and understand the "true" needs, desires, and wants of their affluent clients.
- **Critical Failure Factor #2: Lack of Technical Knowledge.** Advisors fail to identify the opportunities to use estate planning strategies that incorporate life insurance.
- **Critical Failure Factor #3: Lack of Implementation Expertise.** Advisors are unable to effectively implement the appropriate estate planning strategies using life insurance.

The balance of this chapter examines these reasons in greater detail.

Critical Failure Factor #1: Lack of Client Knowledge

Advisors Fail to Uncover and Understand the "True" Needs and Wants of Their Affluent Clients

Unfortunately, this is a pervasive problem throughout the private wealth industry. A spectrum of advisors, from private client lawyers and money managers to accountants and trust officers, repeatedly make recommendations that miss the mark because they haven't taken the time to understand their affluent clients and craft a solution that fits. We conducted two separate studies to better understand this predicament; one was conducted with the estate planning clients of private client lawyers and the other was conducted with the wealthy prospects of investment advisors.

Once an estate plan has been designed and approved, the next step is implementation—but many clients put the process on hold at this stage even though they were involved all along and have paid the bills for the attorney's time and expertise. To identify the reasons behind this behavior we constructed a sample of 288 wealthy families that had engaged a private client lawyer to design an estate plan but had not followed through with the implementation.

A number of reasons were cited, with the most universal being a perception that the estate plan did not satisfy their goals, wants, and objectives. A similarly high number of families said they felt uneasy with the attorney who created the plan and roughly half of survey respondents said they put on the brakes because they were uncomfortable or nervous with the thought of putting the plan into action (Exhibit 4.1). All of these concerns could be allayed if the private client lawyer had asked questions, listened carefully to responses, further probed the topics that elicited a strong reaction, recapped his understanding to the client before proceeding with plan development to ensure they were both on the same page, and helped the client feel as if they had input and influence in the process.

Essentially the same core reason was at the heart of the disconnection between investment advisors and their wealthy prospects. In a study with 103 investors with at least $5 million in investable assets we learned that many investment advisors fail to really understand their prospects before putting forth suggestions and solutions. All of our survey participants had met with and received proposals from investment advisors they did not hire. Their reasons for not doing so are illuminating.

Of the 103 investors, 86.7% said their advisor did not understand them (Exhibit 4.2). A similarly high percentage (85.7%) thought the recommendations from the investment advisor was off track. Yet only a handful (4.3%) said that they did not understand the recommendations, so it wasn't a matter of being baffled; they simply knew enough to realize that the recommendations were not right for them.

EXHIBIT 4.1
Rationale for Not Implementing an Estate Plan

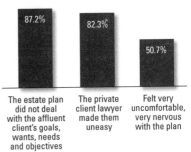

| The estate plan did not deal with the affluent client's goals, needs and objectives | The private client lawyer made them uneasy | Felt very uncomfortable, very nervous with the plan |

N = 288 affluent clients
Source: The Private Client Lawyer; Now and in the Future (Wealth Management Press, 2003)

EXHIBIT 4.2
Why Investment Advisors Didn't Land Affluent Prospects as Clients

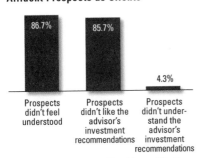

| Prospects didn't feel understood | Prospects didn't like the advisor's investment recommendations | Prospects didn't understand the advisor's investment recommendations |

N = 103 investment prospects with a minimum of $5 million in investable assets
Source: Wealth Management (Wealth Management Press, 2003)

If the majority of affluent clients do not feel understood, there is something lacking in the discovery process being used by advisors and other professionals. It is equally sobering that many of the wealthy do not agree with the recommendations coming from their estate planning and advice professionals. All affluent clients want to be comfortable with the professional who will handle their financial and legal affairs, including their estate plan—but today that is clearly not the case.

The lesson derived from these studies can be directly applied to the use of life insurance in estate planning situations. No matter how brilliant or tax-efficient a strategy is, if it does not resonate with your clients because it doesn't reflect their needs and desires, no further action will be taken. A persistent lack of client information can have a deeper and more destructive impact on a relationship, but can be remedied with the use of a systematic and proven profiling mechanism. This process, called the Whole Client Model, is the subject of Chapter 5.

Critical Failure Factor #2: Lack of Technical Knowledge

Advisors Fail to Identify the Opportunities to Use Estate Planning Strategies that Incorporate Life Insurance

For many advisors, life insurance is something of a mystery and they readily acknowledge their limited understanding of the product and its uses. We questioned 1,561 advisors who provide estate planning services as part of their offering about their knowledge of the strategies that incorporate life insurance (Exhibit 4.3). Less than one-quarter of respondents consider themselves highly knowledgeable. High-end life insurance agents (with consistent annual incomes >$300,000) focused on wealth transfer are the most knowledgeable at nearly 50%, while all other groups are represented at much lower levels.

It became clear during the open-ended portion of the interviews conducted as part of this study that advisors will identify themselves as highly knowledgeable if they have in-depth knowledge of a single strategy. In fact, very few advisors have a broad-based understanding of the uses of life insurance in estate planning.

EXHIBIT 4.3
Highly Knowledgeable about Estate Planning Strategies Incorporating Life Insurance

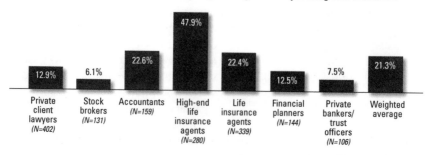

This conclusion is reinforced when we consider that nearly three-quarters of the advisors surveyed are interested in learning how life insurance can be used in estate planning (Exhibit 4.4). Excepting private bankers and trust officers, all other types of advisors responded in the majority.

Part III: The Role of Life Insurance in Estate Planning of this book provides detail

EXHIBIT 4.4
Interested in Learning About Estate Planning Strategies Incorporating Life Insurance

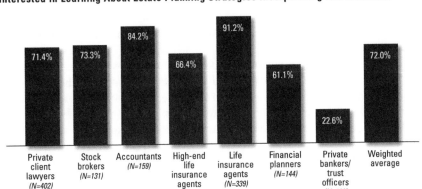

Private client lawyers (N=402)	Stock brokers (N=131)	Accountants (N=159)	High-end life insurance agents (N=280)	Life insurance agents (N=339)	Financial planners (N=144)	Private bankers/ trust officers (N=106)	Weighted average
71.4%	73.3%	84.2%	66.4%	91.2%	61.1%	22.6%	72.0%

and practical examples that will help bridge the knowledge gap identified above. However, wealth managers do not need to be estate planning or life insurance experts. Instead, the goal is to consistently recognize fact patterns in affluent client situations, spot opportunities, and know when to summon a life insurance specialist.

Critical Failure Factor #3: Lack of Implementation Expertise

Advisors are Unable to Effectively Implement the
Appropriate Estate Planning Strategies using Life Insurance

The completion of a life insurance sale is a complex process that can pose a number of obstacles to a professional who is not familiar with its many facets. The seven issues listed below are the most common issues that derail the implementation process.

- Not understanding what is involved to implement the estate planning strategy.
- Not having the right documents drafted properly.
- Not selecting the appropriate insurance carrier(s).
- Not being attuned to the underwriting process.
- Not selecting the appropriate product.
- Not managing the reinsurance process.
- Not leveraging assets to mitigate funding costs.

Even the most basic estate planning strategies that use life insurance require regulatory, structural, and product knowledge. Knowing the rating, reputation, and capabilities of insurance companies will help guide the carrier selection process, and a familiarity with reinsurance and the interdependencies and responsibilities of all the involved parties will make any process run more smoothly. Without any of this knowledge it is impossible for a wealth manager to know the effect each decision and action will have on other parts of the process—and can result in anything from impediments to full-scale breakdown.

A high-quality life insurance specialist will have the experience and expertise needed to manage implementation for you and your wealthy clients. In other words, this issue can be resolved by working with the right partner and guidelines for evaluating and choosing a life insurance specialist are the subject of Chapter 6.

Implications

There are three primary reasons that advisors fail to see insurance opportunities in their books of business—myopic knowledge of their clients, a limited understanding of the strategies that use life insurance, and an inability to shepherd the implementation process. Consequently, many high-net-worth individuals that would benefit from the product are never approached and a number of opportunities are left idle. All of these deficiencies can be easily addressed with the incorporation of new tools and techniques and a working partnership with the right life insurance expert.

CHAPTER 5

■

THE WHOLE CLIENT MODEL

At the core of wealth management—and your success as a wealth manager—is the depth, breadth and quality of the information you have about your clients. Irrespective of the products you offer or how you are remunerated for your expertise, the starting point for any new strategy (including estate planning strategies that use life insurance products) is a framework of information that allows you to evaluate its fit and appropriateness against your client's financial agenda.

A client profile is the single most valuable tool in a professional services business. We have found that profiling individuals before they become clients can help advisors in a variety of ways. It sets expectations with the client about the way an advisor works and the level of detail they need to do their job. It also provides a solid base of knowledge that can be used to tailor proposals and recommendations, and later as a springboard for expansion. And since clients aren't static, their profiles shouldn't be either. It is important to update a client's profile throughout the course of a relationship to be certain that all the relevant aspects have been identified. And major events—such as births and adoptions, IPOs, death, divorces, sales and mergers of businesses, residential purchases, major gifts to charity, and retirement—should automatically trigger an update because a wealth manager is only as effective as the information they possess about their clients.

The best profiles are the most detailed and include things such as client needs, wants, facts, figures, attitudes, perceptions, preferences, personal and professional relationships, social dynamics, and thought processes. Many advisors may not have the experience needed to question their clients about areas outside the scope of investments and finances, but will need to push themselves outside their comfort zone in order to evolve as professionals and maximize their affluent client relationships.

A Comprehensive Profiling Approach

Most profiling tools require extensive detail on narrowly defined areas of the client's state of affairs, usually assets and finances. This is a good start, but insufficient since it overlooks the components of a wealthy client's personal and professional situations that can affect the solutions an advisor might propose.

Some of you may be familiar with our research on the Elite 1200—these are the nation's most successful advisors, those practitioners who have demonstrated consistent earning in excess of $1 million annually (before taxes, after expenses). Over several years we analyzed the business models and practices of the Elite 1200 to determine what they did differently from, and better than, their less successful counterparts. All members of the Elite 1200 rely on some form of fact-finding effort to construct a client profile. We developed a composite of their questions and integrated it with empirical analysis of longitudinal high-net-worth data to develop a more accurate, perceptive, actionable, and comprehensive profiling mechanism—the Whole Client Model.

The Whole Client Model is comprised of seven categories that together represent a complete picture of a wealthy individual. They are: client vitals, financials, relationships, advisors, process, interests, goals and concerns. The following is the seven-sector framework of the Whole Client Model and some sample questions a wealth manager might use to prompt conversation about, and extract information on, each of the topics.

Client Vitals
- What is the client's age?
- What is the client's total net worth?
- What is the client's gender?
- What is the client's income?
- What is the client's high-net-worth personality?

Financials
- What does the client's investment portfolio look like today?
- How are the non-investible assets structured?
- How does the client make money today? How is that likely to change in the next three years?

- How does the client save or set aside money to invest? How is this likely to change in the next three years?
- What benefits does the client receive from his or her workplace?
- What life insurance does the client have?
- What property does the client have (e.g., real property, art, jewelry, etc)?
- What new assets does the client expect to receive (e.g. inheritances, stock options) and when?
- What is the client's opinion on taxes? What kinds of taxes bother the client the most?
- What are his or her three biggest worries about his or her investment portfolio?
- What were the client's best and worst investments? What happened?
- What is the client's debt situation?

Relationships

- What family member relationships (spouse, children, brothers, sisters, parents, et al.) are the most important ones? Are any family members important in the client's professional life?
- What is the client's religious orientation? How devout is he or she?
- What pets does the client have? How important are these pets?
- How important are the relationships with the people the client works with?
- How important to the client are relationships with people in his or her community?
- Would the client describe him or herself as an introvert or extrovert?
- What famous people does the client know? How did he or she meet them?
- What schools did the client go to? How important is his or her relationship with these schools?

Advisors

- Who are the other advisors the client is using? What role does each play?
- How frequently has the client switched advisors?
- What was the client's best and worst experience with an advisor?
- Does the client have a trusts-and-estates lawyer? How does he or she feel about the relationship?
- Does the client have a life insurance agent? How does he or she feel about the relationship?
- Does the client have an accountant? How does he or she feel about the relationship?
- Does the client have investment advisors? How does he or she feel about these relationships?

- Does the client have a financial planner? How does he or she feel about the relationship?

Process

- How many contacts are optimal for the client? Investment-oriented contacts? Non-investment-oriented contacts?
- What security measures is the client using to protect his or her personal and financial information?
- Who else needs to be involved in the planning process for the client?
- How many face-to-face meetings would the client want over the course of a year?
- Would the client want a call from you when there is a sudden change in the market?
- Does the client want e-mail contacts from you? What should the e-mail contacts be about?
- How often does the client want an overall review of his or her financial situation and progress towards goals?

Interests

- What are the client's favorite activities, TV programs, movies, and sport teams?
- Are health and fitness important to the client? If so, what is his or her regimen?
- What charitable causes does the client donate to? Does he or she volunteer?
- What does the client enjoy reading?
- What are the client's hobbies?
- What would the client's ideal weekend be?
- What would an ideal vacation be?

Goals and Concerns

- What are the client's lifestyle desires? (e.g., houses, travel, boats, cars?)
- What does the client consider his or her top accomplishments to be? What would he or she like them to be?
- What are the client's personal goals? What is of central importance to the client personally?
- What keeps the client up at night? In other words, what worries the client?
- What are the client's professional goals (short and long-term)?
- What does the client do for his or her children? What does the client want to do?
- What does the client do for his or her parents? What does the client want to do?
- What does the client do or want to do for other family members or close friends?
- What does the client want to do for society, for the world at large?

- Ideally, where would the client like to be when he or she is 45? And then at age 55, 65, and 75?
- What are the client's investment goals? In dollar figures, how much money does he or she need or want?
- If the client did not have to work anymore, what would he or she do?

The ideal way to capture and present the information gathered as part of the Whole Client Model is as a real-time schematic meaning as the details are communicated they are used to fill in the diagram (Exhibit 5.1). The advantages to using a graphic approach include:

- Being able to review the client on a single piece of paper
- More rapid and effective organization of data
- Obvious interdependencies between specific areas in a client's life
- Ability to spotting redundancies and deficiencies in products, services, and details
- Emerging fact patterns based on multiple pieces of information
- Creating a tool that can facilitate conversations with the experts and specialists in your wealth management network.

EXHIBIT 5.1
The Whole Client Model

The Whole Client Model is a systematic approach to gathering client information that will help an advisor conceptualize their client's agenda and develop an appropriate service model and plan of action.

Garnering the Information

Completing the Whole Client Model exercise means gathering a significant amount of information, perhaps much more than the average advisor is used to collecting from any individual. Many advisors tell us that they feel the number and type of questions required for the Whole Client Model are intrusive or offensive. We do not agree, as most wealthy clients are willing to share the details that help an advisor see them as a unique entity and approach them accordingly. We do, however, agree that adroit questioning techniques are required to accomplish this and a heightened sensitivity to a client's discomfort is also necessary.

Furthermore, every advisor can and should gather all the information they need through one-on-one interactions. Simply handing the client a questionnaire to complete at home defeats the purpose of the exercise, as does reading questions from a form, as it curbs the personal, consultative quality of the interaction. Advisors should educe the information (over time, if necessary) by engaging their affluent clients in discussions about themselves, their needs, and their interests. Discreet note-taking is appropriate, but any meetings should take the form of a conversation, not an interrogation.

Skillful questioning of a client can accomplish more than one objective it will result in an answer, but can also provide insights about a client's knowledge level and sophistication, biases, analytical skills, decision-making process, and willingness to take action. The following types of questions should be considered when preparing to conduct the Whole Client Model:

- **Obtain information.** These questions jog the affluent client's memory and motivate them to share.
- **Test comprehension.** To ensure informed decisions, it is essential for clients to fully understand the issues, alternatives, and implications of any decision. Questions that result in client rephrasing, interpreting, comparing, and detailing can accomplish this objective.
- **Require analysis and evaluation.** Frequently, affluent clients are faced with circumstances and problems that are thorny and carry fiscal and psychological consequences. Many times the best solution involves a compromise or trade-off and an advisor must be able to help the client carefully examine the situation and understand the possible outcomes before taking action.
- **Move the process forward.** Questions are more effective than assertions when the goal is action, since it places control in the client's hands and forces them to acknowledge their priorities.

Lessons From the Field

Most of our coaching and training efforts with advisors include some degree of focus on the Whole Client Model. With appropriate commitment and practice, any advisor or professional can become proficient at using the Whole Client Model. To help abbreviate that process, we have identified the most common oversights of inexperienced practitioners.

Client Vitals
- Not capturing net worth information and only looking for liquid assets.
- Forgetting to identify the exceptionally wealthy client's high-net-worth personality.

Financials
- Not identifying all the assets.
- Not identifying the liabilities.

Relationships
- Failing to look outside the client's immediate family for relationships.
- Failing to identify past marriages or grown children that may no longer be part of the client's day-to-day life and responsibility.

Advisors
- Not getting any details about the other advisors.
- Not finding the degree to which these other advisors are still relevant.

Process
- Not delving deep enough into the way they process information.
- Not finding out whom in their world can expedite or derail progress.

Interests
- Not determining their charitable activities even if it's only "checkbook" philanthropy.
- Not probing enough to identify personal interests even if the affluent client is a workaholic.

Goals and Concerns
- Misreading or misinterpreting goals.
- Failing to help identify key concerns.

The Rationale

In the context of this book, the Whole Client Model is the process wealth managers will use to unearth the details that can reveal the fact patterns that become estate planning needs. These needs are then addressed in the development of an estate plan that will require life insurance in order to implement the strategies.

Like many highly technical subjects, estate planning can be accomplished in a number of ways and even subtle variations in the interpretation of regulations, the structure of legal entities, and the application of products can offer different benefits and results. Skilled use of the Whole Client Model can yield a highly personalized portrait of a client that should be used by the wealth manager and his specialists to select the estate planning approaches that best fit the client's goals, preferences and individuality. The closer the plan and its recommendations are to addressing a client's priorities, the more likely it is to resonate with them and be embraced.

The logic behind the seven categories in the estate planning process is as follows:

- **Client Vitals** provides key demographic information about the affluent individual that provides the basis for an estate plan.
- **Financials** identifies the structure, registration, and location of assets around which an estate plan is crafted, as well as existing plans, policies, and liabilities that should be considered during the process.
- **Relationships** reveals the people who are most important to the client and those who carry some financial or emotional obligation. It may also provide a general sense of the client's wishes for an estate plan and who should participate in the planning process.
- **Advisors** will uncover other professionals who work with the client on a regular basis, including accountants, attorneys, and business managers, and who should be involved in the development of the estate plan. It may also clarify the role and the influence each has in the client's life.
- **Process** identifies the client's preferred method and frequency of interaction, and the level of detail required to satisfy the client's sophistication and curiosity. The introduction of estate planning and life insurance specialists, and any recommendations or documents should be done in accordance with these preferences for maximum effectiveness.
- **Interests** are those activities and topics that occupy the client's time and money, including hobbies, religious, political, medical, and philanthropic, and often prove instrumental in crafting an estate.
- **Goals and Concerns** will include the client's personal and professional goals and their intentions for their family and loved ones, all of which should shape the estate plan in the client's perspective.

When used properly, the Whole Client Model can increase the likelihood that estate planning recommendations are accepted, approved, and implemented – including life insurance, when appropriate.

As demonstrated, the Whole Client Model can help advisors uncover a range of client priorities, concerns, and needs that fall outside the strict scope of estate planning but may require some related strategies and services to be addressed effectively. One such discipline is asset protection, another element of advanced planning that helps an individual shield their wealth from unwelcome overtures such as litigants and creditors, and is sometimes done in conjunction with estate planning to ensure solid results and maximum tax-efficiency. See *Appendix D: Asset Protection* for more information.

Implications

Knowing as much as possible about your wealthy clients is a step toward higher-quality interactions and more targeted communications and recommendations. Having detailed knowledge also means that a client's needs and deficiencies are apparent and can be addressed in a timely fashion. The Whole Client Model is a systematic, proven way to periodically gather critical information about clients that can form the basis for any relationship and help spur the estate planning process. The Whole Client Model, and other similar practices, is at the center of most successful wealth management businesses. In the context of wealth management, estate planning, and life insurance, the Whole Client Model can help an advisor identify estate planning needs, keep the process moving forward, and facilitate the delivery of strategies and solutions based on sound thought and suitable products.

THE ROLE OF LIFE INSURANCE IN ESTATE PLANNING

CHAPTER 6

■

THE USES AND FUNDING OF LIFE INSURANCE

The versatility of life insurance in estate planning can be compared to a Swiss Army Knife. Even the most basic model has many uses and applications—flossing teeth, snipping thread and opening bottles, among them. And like that highly recognizable tool, life insurance cannot do everything, and in certain cases may be a workable but subordinate product. Just think about whether you'd rather use a pocketknife or an 8" Henckels chef's knife to butcher a whole chicken and you'll get the point.

There are many tools, techniques, and strategies available to the professional advisor that can be used in place of or in concert with life insurance. When employed properly and constructively, life insurance can be very effective for affluent clients. It's critical to remember that *people don't buy life insurance to have life insurance, they buy it for what it does* so it should always be introduced and discussed in the context of an overarching plan and a client's personal goals so there is no confusion about its purpose.

The Results of Life Insurance

Life insurance provides three essential results that allow it to be both a solver of problems and a creator of opportunities. They are:

■ **Liquidity.** Upon death, the life insurance policy automatically converts to cash and therefore allows for flexibility in estate administration and post-mortem planning.

■ **Leverage.** With respect to the wealthy, the relationship between premium dollars paid and insurance proceeds received often favors the insured. In other words, there is usually more money paid at death than was paid during life in premiums

■ **Certainty.** Presuming the life insurance has been properly structured and serviced; the proceeds will be there regardless of when the insured dies.

In general, the financial community has a bias toward using life insurance as a solution. Nevertheless, the adroit use of life insurance can result in opportunities that are both powerful and attractive. These scenarios, however, require greater vision on the part of the wealthy client and his or her advisors.

The more common uses of life insurance are discussed below, and a selection of case studies that demonstrate how life insurance is effectively employed in each of these situations can be found in Chapters 7 and 8. There are many uses for life insurance in the context of estate planning and the following 14 objectives should not be considered an exhaustive list of its applications.

Solving Problems

Conceptually, there are eight broad issues where life insurance can prove useful. They are:

1. **Estate liquidity.** Provide cash so that assets do not have to be sold.

2. **Estate equalization.** When other estate assets are not being distributed equally, life insurance can be used to equalize the amounts among all the beneficiaries (such as when one beneficiary gets property like a business interest that is worth far more than the assets left to distribute among the other beneficiaries).

3. **Income with respect to a decedent.** Prevent erosion of assets that are subject to income taxes after death as well as estate taxes, such as royalties, other revenue streams that continue after the individual's death like renewal commissions, as well as various retirement accounts.

4. **Create tax-advantaged income.** Provide an income stream by converting non-income producing assets into income producing assets. Usually accomplished by employing charitable split interest trusts such as charitable lead or charitable remainder trusts.

5. **Transferring concentrated stock positions to heirs.** Making sure that heirs do not have to sell stock at the wrong time while having the benefit of a step-up in basis for the stock.

6. **Employee Stock Ownership Plan liquidity.** Provide funds to be able to cash out participants' accounts.

7. Business continuity. Ensuring that the business will be able to continue by providing funds needed in the event of the death(s) of senior management through key person insurance and/or by funding business transfer agreements.

8. Address multiple marriage issues. A way to provide for children from more than one spouse and to provide for a spouse, especially in conjunction with pre- and/or post-nuptial agreements.

Creating Opportunities

In addition, there are six broad scenarios where life insurance can prove beneficial and accretive. They are:

1. Take advantage of the differential between gift taxes and estate taxes. This arbitrage opportunity can result in significant tax savings.

2. Keeping the estate intact. To pay taxes for the estate rather than from the estate so that what the beneficiaries receive is equal to the total amount for the estate before death. This is an opportunity because many affluent individuals and, unfortunately, many professional advisors don't see the estate erosion as a problem.

3. Allow for a zero tax estate. Ensure there are no estate taxes on the wealth of an individual at death.

4. Create a family bank. Provide a pool of assets available to descendants for an extended time into the future—possibly forever.

5. Support other estate planning techniques. The success of other estate planning techniques may be dependent upon the donor of a gift or the buyer and/or seller of assets surviving a period of time. If the seller of an asset becomes a creditor in that payments are going to be made over time that relies upon the buyer being able to make those payments. In both cases, life insurance provides a hedge against a death while the transaction is in process. Such transactions include:

a. Grantor Retained Annuity Trusts.

b. Self-canceling installment notes.

c. Loans to finance purchase of assets.

6. Charitable giving. Making a gift to charity or to replace the cost of assets donated to charity, especially if using charitable split interest trusts such as charitable lead or charitable remainder trusts.

Funding Strategies

The next hurdle, once a clear link has been made between a client's agenda and the appropriate life insurance policy, is cost. The premiums for life insurance can be steep, and in most cases they must be paid in order to realize a benefit. It's important to know that *people don't object to life insurance, but they object to paying for it* so identifying funding sources for your client that will not adversely affect his or her lifestyle can help clinch the deal.

One of the first areas that seasoned estate planners and life insurance agents will explore is colloquially known as the "bottom of the pile." These are assets, usually liquid, that affluent clients will probably never use during their lifetime—and they know it. Most frequently they are in fixed income investments, such as CDs or municipal bonds, or in retirement vehicles like annuities or IRAs. Learning more about affluent clients as discussed in *Chapter 5: The Whole Client Model* will increase the likelihood that premium dollars can be found.

Successful funding strategies require creativity, an in-depth knowledge of the client, and an understanding of how different assets work and this is especially so with larger premiums. The constraints of gift taxes and any lifestyle requirements can mean that how a premium is funded can be as important to a client as what the insurance will be used to accomplish. The most common funding strategies include:

■ **Cash gifts.** Presuming the life insurance is to be out of the estate, gifts can be made to the owner or beneficiaries (in the case of a trust) to pay premiums.

■ **Gifts or sales of income producing assets.** Gifting or selling assets such as real estate that produce cash flow thereby enabling the purchaser or recipient of the gift to use the cash flow to pay premiums.

■ **Split-dollar.** Loaning or advancing money to the policy owner to pay premiums with the loans or advance secured by the life insurance policy.

■ **Premium financing.** Borrowing money from an outside lender to pay premiums—usually by offering the life insurance policy and other assets as collateral.

■ **Compensation.** In situations where there is a business, a bonus is provided to the owner of the policy that will be used to pay premiums.

■ **Dividends.** When someone has undistributed profits from a C corporation, based on the current tax laws regarding dividends, having dividends with minimal income tax consequences paid to shareholders so that the proceeds can be used to pay premiums.

■ **Previously taxed S Corporation, partnership, or LLC income.** Often times in these pass-through entities there is cash in the entity that has already been taxed. Distributing some of that cash has no income tax consequence and can be used to pay premiums.

■ **Transition from existing life insurance.** Apply the monies being used to pay the premiums on an existing policy or even the cash value of the policy to obtain a superior life insurance policy. This would also apply to moving from a problematic

policy to a more viable alternative.
 — Life insurance/annuity arbitrage which entails benefiting from the difference between a single premium immediate annuity.
 — Life insurance policy and life settlement arbitrage which involves selling a
life insurance policy and purchasing another one providing greater benefits
and/or lower costs.

■ **Annuity trusts.** The income from the remainder trusts and/or the remainder
interest from any annuity trusts can be used to fund premiums.

■ **Unitrusts.** Using the income from the remainder trusts and/or the remainder
interest from Unitrusts to fund premiums.

■ **Utilize funds from existing entities.** Employing the funds in existing trusts and/
or existing "business-purpose" entities or the income generated by these entities
to purchase life insurance.

■ **Distributions from retirement plans.** Since these distributions are income with
respect to decedent items and subject to both an estate and an income tax, it is
sometimes worthwhile to use the income stream to pay premiums.

Additional Considerations

The source of the money that will be used to cover premiums can have some
short-term and long-term implications for a client that should be considered as
part of the funding process. Ideally, the final solution will minimize additional
costs and work harmoniously with the client's broader planning and financial initiatives. They are:

Tax consequences. The money used to pay life insurance premiums may be subject to taxes. Using compensation, for instance, will necessitate paying income tax
and gifted assets may carry gift or generation-skipping taxes. It's common knowledge that high-net-worth individuals are highly sensitive to tax-related issues; unexpected tax obligations will not be appreciated and could derail the implementation of an estate plan. Any concerns or potential issues should be outlined in
advance to your client, so you can prepare together accordingly.

Effects on other planning. As mentioned previously, estate planning should be
undertaken as part of a broader planning initiative rather than as a discrete event.
This will ensure that any byproducts of the process will have a neutral or additive
effect on other planning efforts, rather than a detrimental one. A good example
to illustrate this point is the use of life insurance trusts to keep the death benefit
out of an estate. If the client gifts the assets to fund the premiums to the trust, it

can impact other planning whether or not the gift itself is a taxable event. Specifically, gifts that are eligible for annual exclusions will be deducted from the lifetime exemption and reduce the amount a client can use for other gifting initiatives. (One exception is direct payments to institutions for education or medical care). With life insurance trusts there is also a disconnect between the annual exclusion amount ($12,000 indexed for inflation) and Crummey powers (the greater of $5,000, not indexed, or 5% of the trust's assets).

Implications

The more an advisor understands how life insurance can be used to achieve specific objectives, the easier it will be to recognize when and where it might fit within a client's financial affairs. Having even a conversant knowledge of both the problems it can solve and the opportunities it can generate will allow an advisor to introduce the concept to their wealthy clients before bringing in the necessary specialists.

Like most financial products, say mutual funds or credit lines, life insurance must have a purpose for a client to give it his or her full consideration and it is here that the role of the wealth manager is pivotal. Given the natural bias many people have against life insurance, advisors should focus on presenting it as part of an overall solution rather than a standalone product. Furthermore, taking the time to understand and identify viable funding strategies for your clients can help diminish any perceived obstacles that may exist and simplify the implementation process.

CHAPTER 7

■

CASE
STUDIES

We often rely on case studies to help our clients understand the power and potential of specific advanced planning strategies. It's important to remember that no two cases are alike, but certain philosophies and approaches can be leveraged in the pursuit of similar goals. The five scenarios outlined briefly below have been simplified for illustrative purposes and include some implicit assumptions, but should provide a clear sense of the primary issues and goals, the actions that were taken and the actual or anticipated results.

It's worth reiterating that each of the solutions presented in this chapter has been developed in response to a unique set of client circumstances and requires an in-depth knowledge of the estate planning and funding techniques discussed to be used effectively.

1. Estate Liquidity

Situation

Mr. and Mrs. Frederick, a couple in their late seventies, have an estate of $25 million that is comprised of:

- $10 million in land
- $7 million in investment real estate
- $5 million in personal real estate and property
- $3 million in liquid assets, $2 million of which is in IRAs

They reside in New Jersey, a state with an inheritance tax over and above the Federal Estate Tax, and have three children and four grandchildren for whom they would like to provide.

Based on current values and the tax law that will be in effect in 2009 (an exclusion of $3.5 million and a 45% Federal tax rate), the second death will generate a Federal estate tax obligation of $9.7 million. Since a good portion of the Frederick's estate is illiquid, the beneficiaries may need to cash-out the IRAs, a transaction that will also subject the assets to income tax at the rate of 22%.

Solution

- Their attorney sets up a Grantor Trust for the benefit of the children and grandchildren, and Mr. and Mrs. Frederick make a one-time gift of $350,000 to the trust using their liquid assets.

- The Frederick's sell a discounted limited partnership interest in their investment real estate valued at $3.5 million to the trust. This will "freeze" the value of the real estate at a discount and eliminate any future appreciation from the estate tax calculation. With a cash-on-cash return of 10%, the real estate interest will produce $350,000 in ordinary income each year that goes to the trust.

- The Fredericks receive a balloon note from the trust for $3.15 million that pays 5.15% in interest on an annual basis (the long-term Applicable Federal Rate at the time). The interest to them will be $164,125 each year, payable outside the trust.

- Because this is a Grantor Trust, the grantor (Mrs. Frederick, because of her longer life expectancy) pays the taxes for the trust's $350,000 in income.

- The trust purchases $5.5 million of second-to-die life insurance with the $185,000 in income left after paying interest on the note.

- At the same time, their attorney sets up an Irrevocable Life Insurance Trust (ILIT) for the benefit of the Frederick's children and grandchildren to which Mr. and Mrs. Frederick make annual tax-free gifts of $78,125. The money is used to purchase $2.5 million of second-to-die life insurance. Keeping the gift amount under their individual annual limits of $84,000 (seven beneficiaries at $12,000 each) they avoid any gift tax consequences and further reducing the size of their taxable estate.

Results

The combination of annual gifts and life insurance allow the Fredericks to reduce the overall size of their taxable estate and create a funding mechanism for their projected estate taxes, allowing their beneficiaries to inherit the maximum amount possible.

Life Insurance Sale
$8 million in second-to-die life insurance

Target Premium (equal to a one-time upfront commission) $250,000

2. Estate Equalization

Situation

Cosima has two adult children and owns a successful apparel design business that has been conservatively valued at $40 million. The business is structured as an S Corporation and Cosima retains 75% ownership, or $30 million. Her daughter, Francesca, is involved in the business and owns the other 25% of the business, or $10 million. Her husband and her son are not actively involved, nor do they have ownership stakes.

For estate planning purposes, Cosima wants to provide equally for her children. Cosima expects her daughter to assume full responsibility of the business upon her death. After estate taxes, the net amount of her business equity would be roughly $15 million. She wants to fund a similar inheritance for her son.

Solution

After speaking with her attorney and other counselors, Cosima implements the following plan:

■ With the help of an outside appraiser, the corporation is recapitalized into voting and non-voting shares and a discount rate of 33.3% is established.

■ Cosima and her husband make an outright gift of $3 million in non-voting shares to their son at a discounted value of $2 million, which will be deducted from their total gift exclusion amount.

■ Cosima's voting shares have a current value of $2 million and will be left to Francesca upon Cosima's death, giving her control of the company.

■ The rest of the business, $25 million in non-voting shares, is placed in a QTIP trust with her husband and children named as equal beneficiaries.

■ The son will use the net after tax distributions from the S Corporation to pay the annual premiums on a $12 million second-to-die life insurance policy on his parents. This type of insurance will delay any tax obligations until the second death.

Results

With these structures, Cosima has reduced the size of her taxable estate and made arrangements for both children to receive a net inheritance of approximately

$15 million—the son's will be comprised of stock in the business and insurance proceeds payable at the time of death, the daughter's in the form of Cosima's remaining equity in the business.

Life Insurance Sale
$12 million in second-to-die life insurance

Target Premium (equal to a one-time upfront commission) $200,000

3. Leaving an Income-Producing Asset

Situation

Mr. and Mrs. Hoffman, both 75 years old, own the rights to several much-beloved plays and musicals that are always in production somewhere in the world. Their accountant estimates that the annual income from these royalties is $1 million and will decrease slowly to $650,000 over the next 15 years. Accounting for the sustained popularity of the properties and future inflation (using a 6% interest rate), the royalties have been given a current value of $11 million. The Hoffmans also have a $5 million rollover IRA, investments and real estate holdings that puts their total estate value at $35 million.

Given the nature of the Hoffman's assets, upon inheritance there will be a sizable estate tax bill but no liquid assets to pay it. Royalties are not transferred as a lump sum value, and while the IRA can be liquidated to pay the estate taxes, such a transaction will trigger the income tax, further reducing the assets. Ideally, the Hoffmans will earmark other liquid assets to be available to pay taxes at the time of death.

Solution

■ The Hoffmans establish an Irrevocable Life Insurance Trust (ILIT) enabling the purchase of a $15 million second-to-die life insurance policy outside their estate using an economic benefit split-dollar arrangement.

■ The benefit is calculated based on the likelihood of Mr. and Mrs. Hoffman dieing in the same calendar year so the taxable benefits are low, approximately $15,000 in the first year.

■ The Hoffmans use their income to make $300,000 in annual out-of-pocket gifts to the ILIT to cover the cost of the economic benefit.

■ After the first death, the benefit is recalculated using the single life rates and increasing the annual cost by roughly 15 times, to $225,000, moving forward.

■ At the same time, the Hoffmans set-up rolling two-year Grantor Retained Annuity Trusts (GRAT) with the ILIT as the remainder beneficiary to ensure there is ample funding for future premiums. By making gifts to the GRAT, the remainder can be zeroed out against their tax obligation using the lifetime gift exclusion.

■ When the first spouse dies, the arrangement will be converted to loan split-dollar, a scenario in which all the previously paid premiums become a loan to the trust to be repaid at death.

■ Annual interest on the loan ($36,000 versus an annual cost of $225,000 under the previous arrangement) can either be paid or accrued. The loan will be liquidated when there are sufficient assets to pay premiums or cover the projected estate tax obligation.

Results
Using life insurance and carefully structured trusts, the Hoffmans create a death benefit of $16 million to cover the projected taxes on their estate, allowing the bulk of their assets to pass to their heirs intact.

Life Insurance Sale
$10 million in second-to-die life insurance

Target Premium (equal to a one-time upfront commission) $300,000

4. Selling Appreciated Property

Situation
Mr. and Mrs. Tobin, a couple in their mid-50s, are shopping their business with the hopes of realizing $15 million in proceeds from the sale. The projected windfall has prompted them to revisit their priorities and update their estate plan. The business is their main source of income and they are concerned about maintaining their lifestyle in retirement. They are also interested in making a substantial gift to a charity that is devoted to treating, curing and preventing multiple sclerosis, a disorder that afflicts their youngest daughter. Lastly, they want to provide for their three children.

Solution
■ The Tobins create a Charitable Remainder Unit Trust (CRUT) with the charity named as the beneficiary.

■ They use their annual and lifetime gift exclusions to make an outright gift of their business to the trust, creating an immediate charitable deduction (see below) and eliminating any income taxes generated by a potential sale.

■ Using the government calculations based on their life expectancy and the IRS

7520 interest rate at the time of transfer, the Tobins can deduct a portion of the transferred value totaling roughly $2.6 million.

- The trust will provide annuitized income to the Tobins for the rest of their lives of 6% of the principal amount payable quarterly. The business is valued at $15 million, so the annual income is $900,000 and will be paid to the Tobins in four quarterly installments of $225,000 each.

- By electing to receive a percentage of the principal each year in the form of income, both the trust's value and the Tobin's payout will change.

- The investment strategy used to manage the assets in the trust projects a 7% annual return. Using those assumptions, the Tobin's payments will increase each year.

- The Tobins set up an ILIT and fund it with $950,000/year for two years using the money they saved in taxes on the sale of their business. By keeping the annual amount under $1 million, the Tobins can avoid gift-related taxes.

- The ILIT purchases $8.25 million of second-to-die life insurance to fund an inheritance for their children (the expected proceeds from the sale of their business after estate taxes). The assets in the trust pay for the policy in just two years.

Results

The Tobins create a meaningful income stream to maintain their lifestyle and an inheritance for their children that is outside their estate and not subject to taxes at the time of the second death. Based on the life expectancies and assumptions outlined above, they will also save a total of $2.25 million in income taxes that would have been due when their company was sold and the multiple sclerosis charity will receive more than $18 million when the CRUT is liquidated.

Life Insurance Sale
$8.25 million in second-to-die life insurance

Target Premium (equal to a one-time upfront commission) $150,000

5. Transferring a Concentrated Stock Position

Situation

Bernard is a vice chairman of a Fortune 500 company. His estate is valued at $40 million, three-quarters of which is in employer stock. Half of his stock, or $15 million, is in restricted units meaning he cannot sell, transfer or gift his shares until they are fully vested. The company is in the midst of a restructuring which has greatly devalued the stock, but Bernard believes it will double in value over time. Upon his death, he would like his children to retain ownership of the stock until it reaches its full potential.

Solution

Bernard wants to use life insurance to cover the $16 million in estate taxes he calculates would be due if he dies in 2009. His current income will not accommodate the annual premiums of $185,000 so he approaches his company for assistance.

■ The company enters into a loan split-dollar arrangement with Bernard. The firm lends money to an ILIT that, in turn, purchases the $16 million life insurance policy and pays the annual premiums.

■ Absent other stipulations for determining the AFR, split-dollar regulations put the term of the loan at seven years, which will establish the interest at a specific rate.

■ Bernard uses his income to pay interest to the company every year on the loan. The interest he pays for the ILIT will be considered a gift, but may not be used against his exclusion.

■ The loan is contingent on Bernard's continued employment, so a longer-term solution is required. Bernard and his estate planning attorney set up a limited partnership using some of his company stock. Initially, Bernard is the only partner.

■ Next, they establish a GRAT and Bernard gifts his stock (now shares in the limited partnership) to the trust at a 30% discount per an outsider appraiser. It is purposely structured so that it has a low value for gift tax purposes and there is a high likelihood that assets will be left over for the next generation after all premiums and loans have been paid in full.

■ The remainder beneficiary is the ILIT.

■ The size of the GRAT is $6.5 million, derived from the projected remainder amount necessary to pay off the loan to the company and continue to pay premiums on the insurance going forward.

Results

Bernard's children will not be negatively impacted by the estate taxes due on their inheritance, and will be able to keep the company stock until it reaches its target valuation.

Life Insurance Sale

$16 million of universal life

Target Premium (equal to a one-time upfront commission) $185,000

CHAPTER 8

■

WORKOUTS

Probably the largest opportunity to provide life insurance to affluent clients is not catering to new wealthy clients, but by "fixing" or "improving" the situations for existing affluent clients – an area of specialization referred to as workouts. There are a panoply of client situations involving life insurance where the astute professional advisor can add tremendous value. This will sometimes necessitate rewriting existing life insurance policies.

At one end of the spectrum there are advanced estate planning strategies that are unequivocally legal. At the other end of the spectrum there is a gray zone where the validity of a given strategy is presently open to interpretation. Then there is the zone where gray has turned to pitch black. This is the dominion where a professional advisor's integrity or lack thereof, becomes readily apparent.

We are increasingly seeing articles in the press calling into question the validity of some advanced estate planning strategies that use life insurance. This trend, in combination with the assault on some tax strategies where the IRS declares them listed transactions, has understandably made many professional advisors and especially their wealthy clients nervous and hesitant.

Abusive Estate Planning Strategies

The question is: "How aggressive is too aggressive?" Abusive estate planning strategies can be very detrimental to everyone involved. Just consider the case of the now illegal advanced estate planning strategy, charitable reverse split dollar.

In charitable reverse split dollar an affluent donor made a contribution to a willing charitable organization of an amount equal to the PS58 costs based on the IRS table for a certain amount of life insurance. The charitable organization would turn around and, in concert with the donor, pay the money to the insurance company as part of the premium for a policy on the life of the donor. The donor then contributed the balance of the premium, an amount considerably less than the amount contributed by the charitable organization. Through a split-dollar agreement, the charitable organization owned the death benefit based on the amount paid in premium using the PS 58 table to determine cost. The donor owned the cash value and could terminate the relationship upon any policy anniversary so that the charitable organization would not receive anything. With this strategy, the donor would receive a tax deduction and owned cash value and life insurance that were of much greater comparative benefit than what had been contributed.

The strategy was actively marketed by a company that provides products and services to the life insurance industry and was accompanied by an opinion letter from an attorney with a prominent law firm. Inevitably, this inventive but questionable strategy attracted government scrutiny. In 1999, under the "partial interest rule", the IRS in Notice 99-36 warned about adverse tax and penalty consequences. Subsequently, in the "Tax Relief Extension Act of 1999," a law was passed to deal with personal benefit contracts and included provisions such that in addition to the taxpayer facing taxes, fines, and penalties, there would be an excise tax imposed on charities that facilitated these transactions. Additionally, any charitable organization that had conducted such a transaction had to file a report with the IRS and there was no grandfathering. The reason for the IRS and the legislative responses were simple enough: the charitable intent on the part of the donor was not present. The strategy also employed an outdated IRS table that has been subsequently revised under IRS Notice 2001-10. Since then, the seemingly straightforward and altruistic relationships between many affluent donors and charitable organizations have been reconsidered, sometimes to the discredit of both parties.

Red Flags

There are a number of "signs" that should give any estate planner pause when it comes to using strategies incorporating life insurance for affluent clients. These "red flags" indicate the need for intense due diligence on the part of the professional advisor. Some of the red flags are:

■ **Does the strategy have clear economic benefit?** Every legitimate advanced estate planning strategy must have "a substantial and material non-tax business purpose." Clearly, any attempt at tax laundering in any shape or form is clearly unacceptable.

■ **Is signing a nondisclosure agreement required?** It's all too common for some providers not to permit perspective affluent clients to submit the advanced estate planning strategies they're proposing to outside review by other advisors. When a prospective client has to sign one of these agreements in order to be "privileged" to learn about a strategy, it is a sure red flag.

■ **Is signing a "hold harmless" agreement required?** The agreement says that the provider of the strategy and/or the life insurance company providing the product is legally not responsible to what happens to the affluent client because of the strategy. Any formal agreement that limits the liability of the provider of an advanced estate planning strategy is a cause for serious concern.

■ **Does the advisor consistently avoid explaining the strategy advocating the need to just trust him or her.** As we noted in *Chapter 2: The State of Estate Planning*, one of the hallmarks of viable advanced estate planning strategies is transparency. When the strategy is a "black box," it often comes with explosives and a timer.

■ **Where is the insurable interest?** On a state-by-state basis, there are clear guidelines for defining an insurable interest. Consequently, when there is not a clear and solid insurable interest as approved by the state in question, the strategy is highly suspect.

When the goal is to benefit charity is charity benefited? Any time a strategy has a charitable component, there must be strong charitable intent on the part of the affluent client and, in the end, the charity must meaningfully benefit.

■ With a best estimate of 671,000 families in the United States with an estate of $10 million or more, commanding $61.7 trillion, there is a considerable opportunity for providing life insurance to pay estate taxes—which, in one form or another, are not going away. For astute and capable professional advisors, there is no need to cross the line. However, the line seems to be crossed with considerable frequency and enthusiasm.

What is required is serious due diligence. Highly aggressive advanced estate planning strategies that use life insurance may be quite innovative and, for a time, quite successful—defined as being adopted by affluent clients. But, that does not mean they should be. Each one must be thoroughly scrutinized from an ethical perspective.

Clearly, there are a minority of advisors and affluent clients whose moral compass is broken. It is incumbent on professional advisors, however, to not employ advanced estate planning strategies that are over the line and, above all, to not employ strategies that may compromise their well-to-do clients. If an affluent client insists on employing such strategies, even after the pitfalls have been pointed out, a professional advisor must weigh ending the relationship.

The Motivation to Cross the Line

Getting caught employing an over-the-line advanced estate planning strategy results in penalties for the affluent clients involved including fines, interest, paying back taxes, and, in a number of the cases, the loss of significant assets. For the professional advisors, getting caught also entails penalties, in some cases the loss of their professional licenses and, more and more often being sued by the affluent clients for malpractice with more and more courts siding with the plaintiffs.

With potential draconian consequences, what motivates professional advisors as well as the wealthy to cross the line? When these parties do a cost/benefit calculation, they conclude that given the amount of money involved, the risk of being caught is deemed worth taking.

Playing the audit lottery is becoming more attractive to a growing number of the affluent. At the same time, the amount of time, energy, and mental firepower that the government can bring to bear is not equal to the resources many affluent clients and their professional advisors can muster. As a result, a select portion of the affluent and their advisors will continue to be over-aggressive because they perceive the benefits outweigh the risks.

While it is incredibly unlikely that the consequences of getting caught will deter all professional advisors, those that care to cross the line are putting themselves in a position where their actions will come back to haunt them. It is up to the professional advisors, through their understanding of the legal consequences and their ethical grounding, to draw the line and know which side to stay on.

As we all know, there are more than a few professional advisors who are ethically challenged and willing to take the chance of getting caught being overly aggressive, sometimes to the point of illegality. While the actions of these advisors may poison the well for everyone, they also set the stage for ethically grounded, technically competent professional advisors. The field of workouts is becoming a fertile field for providing life insurance, and it's where we turn to now.

We are now dealing with a new environment of heightened awareness, anger, tougher laws, and greater oversight and enforcement. The backlash can be detrimental to affluent clients and their professional advisors. Many wealthy clients are concerned about the negative consequences of things they have already done. Many are anxious about achieving their objectives. For a growing number of them, their confidence in their professional advisors has been shaken.

At an increasing rate, affluent clients that have implemented advanced estate planning strategies, particularly those that are complicated and/or opaque, are looking for second opinions. We are also seeing that wealthy clients in greater numbers are seeking second opinions on new proposals.

Unethical professional advisors are one of the two main drivers of the explosion in workouts. The other main driver is the seemingly perpetual changes impacting the estate planning environment and the world of life insurance. From changing tax laws and regulations to the ingenuity of professional advisors to the evolution in insurance products, there is a multitude of opportunities for making "things better" for the affluent client by "fixing" or "improving" an advanced estate planning strategy or life insurance policy.

To better understand the possibilities, let us focus on two scenarios. First we will look at split dollar as an example of the opportunity that comes about because of changing rules. Then we will examine trust owned life insurance as an example of what can be accomplished because today's life insurance products tend to be superior to earlier life insurance products.

Fixing Split Dollar Plans

In *Chapter 6: The Uses and Funding of Life Insurance* we discussed what these plans are, how they work, and the current regulations. All split dollar plans should be examined because of the potential significant adverse consequences to wealthy clients brought about by regulatory changes.

With such consequences facing affluent clients coupled with the fiduciary responsibility of their professional advisors, it would be wise for these clients to be contacted so that their split dollar arrangements can be fixed. To evaluate this situation we surveyed 727 professional advisors on the topic. The professional advisors included private bankers/trust officers, life insurance agents, private client lawyers, and accountants.

First we had to determine if the change in split dollar regulations meant anything to these advisors. In effect, do they have affluent clients who have split dollar arrangements? As it turned out, almost 70% of the professional advisors did have clients with split dollar arrangements (Exhibit 8.1). Another 12.9% did not. More telling was that 18.7% did not know if their affluent clients had split dollar arrangements.

EXHIBIT 8.1
**Have Clients with
Split Dollar Arrangements**

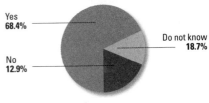

Yes
68.4%

Do not know
18.7%

No
12.9%

N = 727 professional advisors

Only considering those professional advisors (N = 497 professional advisors) who have clients with split dollar arrangements, the issue now becomes what has the professional advisor done in the face of their fiduciary responsibility coupled

EXHIBIT 8.2
Contacted Clients Who Have Split Dollar Arrangements

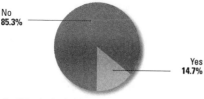

No
85.3%

Yes
14.7%

N = 497 professional advisors

with the changes in the regulations concerning split dollar. Specifically, has the professional advisor contacted their clients to discuss the changes in the split dollar regulations and what their options are? As it turns out, only 14.7% of the advisors surveyed have indeed contacted their clients (Exhibit 8.2). The vast majority of advisors (85.3%) have not.

If we conclude that it is the fiduciary responsibility of the professional advisor to correct planning problems, then why have so few of the advisors surveyed taken the initiative? We have found two interrelated reasons for their professional inaction. One has to do with the fact that relatively few of the professional advisors who have clients with split dollar arrangement (18.1%) have a detailed understanding of the current regulations concerning split dollar (Exhibit 8.3).

The second reason (which is totally correlated to the first) is that only 13.1% of the professional advisors who have clients with split dollar arrangements believe they are knowledgeable and capable of properly "fixing" them (Exhibit 8.4). We define "fixing" a split dollar arrangement as not merely unwinding one,

EXHIBIT 8.3
Have a Detailed Understanding of the New Split Dollar Regulations

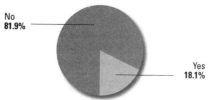

No
81.9%

Yes
18.1%

N = 497 professional advisors

EXHIBIT 8.4
Knowledgeable and Capable of "Fixing" Split Dollar Arrangements

No
86.9%

Yes
13.1%

N = 497 professional advisors

but restructuring the strategy with the intent of ensuring—if desired—the client continues to reap the benefits of the split dollar arrangement in the current regulatory environment.

Contrary to the impression given by some insurance companies and practitioners, there is no single optimal "Split Dollar Rescue Plan." The answer to the question: "What do I do now?" is: "It depends." Moreover, we advocate that the professional advisors who have affluent clients with split dollar plans should take corrective actions, both to maintain the affluent client's goodwill and to head off any potential liability. In the four-step process many factors have to be gleaned and then taken into account:

- ■ **Step 1**: A situational assessment (accomplished by employing the Whole Client Model) that includes:
  - — Evaluate the client's current agenda.
  - — Evaluate the client's current estate plan.
  - — Evaluate the client's financial situation.
  - — Identify sources for premium dollars.
  - — Determine the client's current insurability.
  - — Evaluate existing insurance policy performance.
  - — Ascertain the mechanics of the split dollar arrangement.
- ■ **Step 2**: Scenario analysis.
  - — Match appropriate preservation methods to the situational analysis results.
- ■ **Step 3**: Confirmation and implementation.
  - — Advisors and the affluent client agree on a strategy.
  - — Specify the steps and timeline.
  - — Implement the "fix."
- ■ **Step 4**: Ongoing servicing.
  - — Monitor the regulatory environment for changes to split dollar.
  - — Ensuring the insurance policy is working properly.
  - — Using the Whole Client Model ensure the affluent client continues to be understood.

There are quite a number of different though interrelated preservation methods that will enable clients to maintain, if not augment, the benefits of their split dollar arrangements. As we noted, to make certain that affluent clients are appropriately served, there is no single best solution. What follows constitutes a small sampling of methods that can be employed to preserve the benefits of split dollar under the current regulatory environment:

- ■ Sell the policy to an entity that is already funded.
  - — This can be a properly structured Family Limited Partnership or an existing trust.
- ■ Do nothing if the insured has a short life expectancy.

- If it is a non-equity arrangement or the crossover point to equity is far in the future, wait and see what develops, but have a rollout strategy already in mind, if not set up.
- Fund the policy so that there will be enough equity to terminate the agreement and continue the insurance in force without further payments.
  — Switch from an economic benefit arrangement to a loan arrangement at the equity crossover point.
- Exchange the policy for another policy that is more efficient using section 1035.
- Terminate the arrangement and enter into a transaction that better suits the current situation.
  — At older ages, an exchange to a single premium immediate annuity may provide the necessary funding to pay premiums on a new policy.
- Allow the equity to accumulate and terminate the arrangement when the accrued equity is sufficient to self-fund the policy. At that point, assuming a grantor trust, the grantor would pay an income tax on the equity and the equity would be a taxable gift to the trust.
- Fund the trust for a rollout.
  — If not generation skipping, a zeroed out Grantor Annuity Trusts or Charitable Lead Annuity Trusts can fund it.
  — If it is generation skipping, consider a sale to a grantor trust or sale of a remainder interest in a Grantor Annuity Trusts.
- Split dollar between trusts that have the same beneficiaries.
  — No gifts if the same beneficiaries, therefore the economic benefit rates become irrelevant.
- Surrender or viaticate if the policy is not going to be continued.

Very often these methods are used in concert with other advanced estate planning strategies. It will all depend on the situation analysis. For example, it is possible to structure a split dollar arrangement with a dynasty trust that does not result in any gifts, generation skipping gifts, or outright premium payments.

By understanding the new rules as well as the multiple ways life insurance can be used, there continue to be a number of ways to serve the affluent client using split dollar arrangements. Thus, with a little bit of creativity, wealthy clients with split dollar arrangements are able to continue to benefit from them as they originally chose to. At the same time, split dollar arrangements will continue to be a very viable planning tool for selected new affluent clients.

In sum, what we can conclude is that there are a substantial number of split dollar plans "out there." Professional advisors who have affluent clients with split dollar plans have a fiduciary duty to these clients to fix them. The complication is that most professional advisors lack the expertise to fix them. Thus, for professional advisors who understand split dollar there continue to be significant workout opportunities.

Fixing Trust Owned Life Insurance

What is the problem with trust owned life insurance? In general, the problem with trust owned life insurance is the problem with all trusts: the fiduciary liability of the trustee. They are fiduciaries towards the beneficiaries—not the grantor with whom they have a relationship. Ultimately, it is those beneficiaries that can hold the trustee responsible.

With what has happened regarding life insurance product performance (premiums that continue beyond the projected self-funding date, and variable life, to name two), new and better products becoming available (lower expenses, death benefit guarantees, mortality changes, underwriting standards changes), changes in estate tax law, and changes in tax law regarding life insurance such as what is happening to split dollar programs, exercising prudent fiduciary responsibility is extremely difficult for a trustee. And because for so many, life insurance itself is a "black box," the trustee usually does not have the knowledge, experience, nor skill to do the proper analysis.

A study conducted with 563 professional advisors—private bankers/trust officers, attorneys and accountants—first determined if they were trustees of life insurance trusts for affluent clients (not family or friends). More than half (52.8%) were trustees (Exhibit 8.5). Nearly all the private bankers/trust officers (97.9%) were trustees while proportionally fewer lawyers (22.8%) and accountants (17.5%) were trustees.

EXHIBIT 8.5
Professionals as Trustees

N = 563 professional advisors

Of those who are trustees, only 16.5% have a formal process of reviewing the life insurance policies in the trusts (Exhibit 8.6). That is, there are stated guidelines and procedures for examining the trust-owned life insurance to ensure it is working to meet the objectives of the trust. While we did not examine the guidelines and procedures being used by these trustees, their existence significantly enhanced the probability that the trust-owned life insurance polices are being effectively monitored and corrected when necessary.

More telling is that the remaining 83.5% of trustees do not have stated guidelines and procedures in place. Therefore, there is a very good chance that a number of these policies are not operating as projected, which can result in them not delivering when the grantor dies. Only 4.7% of trustees had life insurance investment policy statements for their trusts.

EXHIBIT 8.6
Advisors Having a Formal Process to Review Trust Owned Life Insurance

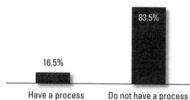

Have a process   Do not have a process

N = 297 professional advisors

We also conducted another study of trust-owned life insurance where a family member or friend was the trustee. This study was of 513 family or friends who are acting as trustees. All the trusts were at least 5 years old with a minimum of $2 million in life insurance (Mean = $9.2 million; Median = $2.7 million). The median age of the trusts was 12.3 years and the mean age of the trusts was 17.1 years. On average there were 2.4 life insurance policies per trust.

Slightly more than a quarter of these trustees (28.8%) had reviewed the life insurance policies within the last 5 years (Exhibit 8.7). Only 5.3% of these trusts had a life insurance investment policy. Another 37.4% of the trustees knew that the trust did not. And, the remaining 57.3% did not know.

A life insurance investment policy statement sets the parameters by which to judge the life insurance in the trust. The grantor may stipulate the purpose of the insurance, the performance goal for the insurance, the quality standards for the company(ies) providing the insurance, the type of insurance to be used (i.e. guaranteed death benefit, variable life), if variable life, the investment policy and hoped for rate of return.

EXHIBIT 8.7
Friends/Family Trustees Reviewed the Life Insurance Policies in the Last 5 Years

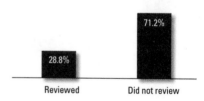

Reviewed   Did not review

N = 513 Family/friends as trustees

There are four steps in reviewing life insurance in an irrevocable life insurance trust:

- **Step 1**: Establish Current Goals.
- **Step 2**: In-force Policy Analysis.
- **Step 3**: Comparative Evaluation.
- **Step 4**: Correct When Necessary.

There is something that needs to be checked before undergoing the review process: Is the trust being properly administered according to its terms? Special attention needs to be given to the Crummey notice provisions and records. Are gift tax returns being filed, and if so, are they consistent with the terms of the trust?

In the first review step it is necessary to determine the current health of the insured(s) and the current overall plan and/or current goals. Once, again employing the Whole Client Model proves highly advantageous.

The in-force policy analysis requires a review of the following:
- The policy terms and riders.
- If variable life, the current investments.
- The policy funding method (i.e. Where does the money come from to pay premiums? Is split dollar being used?).
- A projection of the policy and funding method as it is currently.

The comparative evaluation involves:
- Considering alternate funding methods (this includes split dollar, or incorporating a Family Limited Partnership, as examples) for the existing policy.
- If variable life, an investment strategy.
- Consider whether there are new policies available to the insured(s) that are more efficient.
- If a new policy would be more efficient and can be obtained, how should it be funded.
- Surrender or sale of the existing insurance.

Based upon the first three steps, if there are to be any corrections, they should be implemented. These steps should all be done on a regular basis, like a medical check-up. At the very least, like a review of an estate plan, this should be done at least every three years.

Implications

Both to correct the problems brought on by the greed and hubris of a relatively small handful of unethical professional advisors and just the fact that change in the form of regulations, product and strategy evolution as well as affluent client agendas is the norm in the world of private wealth, the ability for estate planners to better serve affluent clients and financially benefit at the same time is becoming pervasive. Workouts are defined as either fixing an advanced estate planning strategy which includes life insurance that is wrong for one reason or another as well as simply improving a situation because of an evolution in the regulatory environment, insurance products, and expertise.

Using delphi analysis, we were able to conclude that fixing or improving existing affluent client situations by rewriting life insurance is a bigger business opportunity than providing life insurance to new affluent clients. However, to do this well brings us back to the issues we raised in Chapter 4: Critical Failure Factors. Professional advisors who seek to benefit from the opportunity workouts provide must know their affluent clients exceedingly well and understand the fact patterns of the various advanced estate planning strategies that use life insurance.

CHAPTER 9

■

PRODUCT AND CARRIER SELECTION

Our focus has been on the uses of life insurance with due attention to ways to fund the premiums. What is also essential is an understanding of the products per se. In effect, the various types of life insurance and the criteria that needs to be considered in selecting a particular type of policy. Along the same lines, selecting the carrier(s) is also extremely important.

Product Selection
There are four factors that determine product choice:
- **Dollars available**
- **Length of time coverage is wanted**
- **Features desired**
- **Risk tolerance.**

As in everything else, these issues are subjective much more than objective. A discussion of each is in order but the discussion is not going to be about specific companies or products.

Dollars Available. These are dollars the client is *willing* to spend for premiums. After all has been said and done (by you), regardless of how long the insurance will be needed, if the client is only willing to pay for term; give the client term. If the client is willing to commit more, make sure they have the appropriate amount of insurance rather than a lesser amount of the appropriate type of insurance. It is better to have a client who is adequately insured than someone who is not a client. A person's acceptance of life insurance and its uses is something that develops over time, a long time.

Length of Coverage. In addition to the dollars available what determines the appropriate coverage is for how long the coverage is needed. In many estate-planning situations, the coverage is needed the day the person dies, *regardless* of when that is. Having the client acknowledge that point is the most important step to putting the correct coverage in place. (And with continuing trends in improved mortality, particularly among the wealthy who can afford the best health care, it behooves the insurance producer to illustrate the projected results for as far out as the carrier's software will allow—usually to age 115 or 120.)

If a client plans on growing other assets that will be liquid to replace the life insurance later on or making transfers that will reduce the tax liability, term insurance for a period longer than the client anticipates (as a safety factor) may be the best way to go. But if it can be shown to the client the advantage of using a "permanent" product to the client's satisfaction and on the client's terms—such as a better net cost if the client survives or a funding plan that makes the cost competitive with term, please do so. In our experience with wealthy people as they get older - they don't want to give up the coverage. Also, even for those with liquid assets to fund estate taxes, more want insurance than don't. If the client ends up going with term insurance, make sure they are aware of the convertibility options for whatever products are being shown.

The Product Selection Process. Regardless of the length of time for the coverage that is chosen because of the myriad types and features available, the factors must be weighed and discussed with the client. The insurance producer should view him/herself as a purchasing agent for the client—a collaborative process rather than an adversarial one. This involves developing the parameters for product selection with the client and then going into the marketplace based on the client's own specific underwriting factors to find the product and company that best meets the criteria.

Product Features. All insurance products have features that are either inherent in the product or can be added on. What follows is a list of many (but not all) of the features offered today:

Term insurance

- Guaranteed premiums for a period of time.
- Convertibility.
- Renewability – if and at what rates.
- Return of premium if death does not occur.

Whole Life

- Base face amount is guaranteed as long as premiums are paid.
- Can have a limited payment policy that is *guaranteed* to be paid up at a certain point.
- Base continuously builds cash surrender value.
- Designed to endow (the cash surrender value equals the base face amount) at some point.
- Cash value can only be accessed by loan while the policy is in force.
- This is called a general account product in that the underlying investments are made by the insurance company and are not specific to any policy. The investments are usually made up of bonds, mortgages, and some securities.
- If participating (produces dividends) those dividends can be used to:
  — Increase the death benefit annually by buying paid-up additional insurance.
  — Increase the death benefit annually by buying term insurance (until the cost of the term insurance outpaces the growth of the dividends, in which case the death benefit goes down).
  — Increase the death benefit by a level amount from the first year by purchasing a combination of paid-up additions and term insurance. This and the next option reduce the premium for the total face amount as opposed to a policy whose death benefit comes just from the base face amount.
  — Increase the death benefit by an increasing amount, with a higher amount commencing immediately in the first year by a purchasing a combination of term insurance and paid up additions.
  — Accumulate with interest (like a savings account).
  — Reduce the *projected* funding period. Those projections are dependent on the insurance company's actual experience regarding expenses, mortality, and earnings—all of which are reflected in the dividends. The actual results are not known until the insured either dies or the policy is surrendered, which means that even if a policy is already projected to be self-funding, a funding requirement can still reappear later.
  — Dividend values can either be withdrawn (surrendered) or borrowed against while still keeping the policy in force.

Universal (Flexible Premium) Life

- The client selects the amount of premium to be paid starting with the minimum required by the policy. The client can vary premium payment amounts and skip them entirely.
- Unless the policy is funded based on guaranteed values or there are secondary guarantees (these are not the same and will be explained below), the continuation of the policy in force is dependent on the amount of the premium payments, the expenses, mortality, and the earnings.
- This is also a general account product in that the underlying investments are made by the insurance company and are not specific to any policy. The investments are usually made up of bonds, mortgages, and some securities.
- The development of policy values and cash surrender values (the policy account value less any surrender charges equals the amount that can actually be realized if the policy is surrendered) is dependent on the same factors as above. Absent a secondary guarantee—usually called no-lapse or death benefit guarantees—if the account value becomes zero, the policy is no longer in force. Mortality charges can be as big or a bigger factor in this than the earnings rate credited.
- As long as there is a cash surrender value, the policy is in force for its base face amount. If someone is terminally ill and has a universal life policy that has a sufficient cash value, the premiums can be discontinued.
- The policy cash surrender value can be accessed either by withdrawal or loan. While both reduce the death benefit pro rata, a withdrawal will have a worse effect on the policy's performance going forward than will a loan since a loan still produces earnings (the interest) and that interest offsets insurance charges while a withdrawal produces no income to do likewise.
- It is not possible to estimate the performance of a universal life policy based solely on the earnings rate. There is another factor that intensifies the result of changes in earnings rate. Since universal life values change monthly based on earnings and expenses and mortality, and the amount of insurance purchased each month in a level death benefit policy is based on the cash surrender value, if earnings are lower than originally projected, the cash value is lower and more insurance has to be purchased. Result—less earning and more expense equals poorer performance. The reverse is also true—greater earning and less expense equals better performance.
- No-lapse or guaranteed death benefit (secondary guarantee) contracts or riders state that as long as the minimum stipulated premium is paid *on or before the premium due date* the policy will continue in force regardless of the cash

value. Often, the illustrations will show no cash value at some time in the future. Many of these will allow a client to make up for the late timing, skipped, or reduced premiums to regain the full guarantee. But since these contracts and riders are priced based on assumed interest, the makeup factor will be greater (sometimes shockingly so) than the amount that previously had not been paid. These benefits can be for a limited period of time or for life.

■ Coverage extension provides that if the policy is in force at age 100 (for the younger life, if more than one insured), the coverage will continue without any further premium payments. The charge for insurance and expenses cease. Extended maturity may only continue the coverage beyond 100 as long as there is cash surrender value. The charge for insurance and expense continues. The policy may also continue indefinitely without charges for expenses or insurance if there is cash value at 100 ($1.00 usually suffices). Regardless of the name given by the carrier to the option, the actual language in the policy tells how this works. It is important to note that there are differences.

■ Like whole life based either on the guarantees or the appropriate secondary guarantee, premiums can be paid for a limited period of time and then the policy death benefit is guaranteed.

■ The *projected* funding period can be reduced, but again is subject to the future results and premiums that were thought to be self-funded may have to be paid. Further, the amount that has to be paid later can be much greater than the amount that was being paid earlier—more so the longer the premium payments are put off.

■ The death benefit options and riders include the following:
— Level death benefit.
— Death benefit increased by policy accumulation value.
— Death benefit increased by premiums paid.
— Death benefits increased by premiums paid plus interest on premiums paid.
— Death benefits increased by an interest factor.
— Some death benefits can be provided by term insurance, reducing the cost for the total face amount as opposed to having the full face amount come from the base policy. That term insurance is priced lower than the insurance used in the base contract and is more susceptible to change depending on actual experience.

Variable Life

■ The underlying investments that produce cash value are selected from among separate accounts and/or the general account (described above). The separate accounts are managed accounts designed exclusively for use in insurance products. Each separate account has a specific investment objective and methodology and the investments are usually stocks and/or bonds. The owner of the policy can choose (based upon account minimums) to invest in any number and combination of the separate accounts.

- Universal Life – Like Universal Life described previously except that the accumulated and cash surrender values are determined by the performance of the selected separate accounts.
  — The performance of those accounts will determine the performance of the policy.
  — Secondary guarantees are available for varying lengths of time and are usually determined by the allocation to the general account.
- Fixed Premium Life
  — Like whole life but without dividends.
  — Results are dependent upon performance of the sub-accounts.

Risk and guarantees

The client's risk tolerance and goals will help determine which products and options to consider from the above.

- If the client wants absolute guarantees, she/he will choose either an all base whole life or a universal life funded based on the guaranteed values.
- Next down on the risk scale are universal life policies (either general account or variable) with secondary guarantees.
- After the above, absent guarantees, the risk is determined by premiums paid. The lower the premium paid the greater the risk regardless of the policy selected.
- Finally, variable life includes market risk as well.
- A subset of above is limiting the premium payment period. It can be:
  — Funded based on absolute guaranteed values for the set period of time.
  — Funded based on secondary guarantees for the set period of time.
  — Funded based on projected results using assumptions as to product performance absent guarantees.

Carrier Selection

After experience with insurance company failures and product performance issues it is necessary to choose insurance carriers with some care. There are generally two criteria to use claims paying ability and historical treatment of policyholders.

The information on claims paying ability can be had from the rating agencies that provide that information:

- A.M. Best, Moody's
- Standard & Poor
- Duff & Phelps
- Weiss

There is a service offered by LifeLink Corporation called VitalSigns that offers that information as well as actual financial information for all the companies in its database. The ratings often reflect the reputation of the carrier in the marketplace.

Please note that this information should be taken into account with all of the other information regarding appropriate product. While the agency system (in which a producer owes her/his primary allegiance to one insurance company or group of insurance companies) tends to limit the carriers and products explored, it is still within the producer's ability to go beyond that system to find the best products for a client. The selection process should be well documented.

Diversification

In the same way that large investors will diversify their portfolio, when purchasing large amounts of life insurance, the same approach should apply unless there is such a large difference between offers such as underwriting concessions. It is often beneficial when working with more sophisticated strategies that may involve using increasing death benefits.

Different combinations of carriers and products can produce different results. And even though it appears that one company's premium is greater than another, it's often worth the additional outlay to have more than one carrier in the mix to provide additional comfort.

Follow-up

In every case, regardless of the product purchased, there should be an annual review. This review should include a product performance review as well as an update on the client's situation and goals. Any variance in the performance from what was originally projected needs to be looked at and reported. The viability of the product versus alternatives that become available should be looked at.

Twenty-five years ago this section on product selection would have been a fraction of the size. The evolution of products, riders, investments, and mortality created the need for much more information.

Special situations

There are other situations that are found when dealing with very wealthy clients that are not common in other life insurance situations. Some are as follows:

- **Private placement life.** A product available when very large premiums are involved in which the money manager and the expense structure are negotiated directly with a carrier—these products are not necessarily superior to commercially available policies, especially when the primary goal is death benefit.
- **Coordinating reinsurers.** In larger cases (based upon the amount to be issued and the amount in force on the insured(s), carriers will often have to get reinsurers involved. If not handled properly and coordinated with the carriers involved, it's very possible not to be able to get the amount of insurance desired and/or the carriers are shut out of the marketplace
- **Borrowing a life.** Either because of the insurability of an individual or because the amount wanted is so large that even with reinsurance, it cannot be obtained, using other insured's in which the beneficiaries have an insurable interest may be useful.
- **Going right to the reinsurers.** When the situations are large enough, it's sometimes wise to skip the carriers and go directly to the reinsurers. This entails the exceptionally wealthy client creating his or her own captive carrier and negotiating a treaty with a reinsurer.

Implications

The process of selecting policies and funding methods is complex and requires a disciplined approach. The factors need to be fleshed out with the affluent client and all the appropriate advisors. The approach needs to be transparent to all the parties involved. And it can't be left on autopilot once it's implemented.

It has been our experience that regardless of the risks a wealthy client takes in other investment and business areas, when it comes to life insurance and estate planning, wealthy people gravitate more towards guarantees. One of the things life insurance can do is provide a high degree of certainty. Affluent clients know there is certainty in death and taxes. Since the purpose of the insurance was to do something, the clients like to know it will get done—at least to the extent that the insurance proceeds are there.

AFTERWORD

Despite best intentions, our research indicates that most advice practitioners don't function as wealth managers. In fact, the majority of advisors focus on just a handful of the products and services their wealthy clients need. As the ranks of wealth management have swelled, we've seen an emphasis on portfolio management that prioritizes investable assets over all others and often leads to lopsided financial solutions. This approach is passable when the markets are strong and investment results meet expectations. The economic downturn, however, has resulted in staggering portfolio losses and an overall reduction in net worth for many individuals and families—circumstances that are less than ideal for investment-oriented strategies and conversations.

As the financial crisis has persisted, the popularity of family office services has increased indicating a desire for the high-touch, comprehensive experience promised by wealth management, and, perhaps, a more balanced approach that will address a broader range of needs while mitigating certain risks.

We know that estate planning and life insurance are two of the more common and pressing needs of the affluent population, and also two of the most overlooked. They are a natural extension of an investment-centered approach and can be easily incorporated into a financial planning discussion. Fortunately, the current environment is an excellent time to broach these subjects. Losses are top-of-mind and clients are open to new ideas that will help them prevent unnecessary risks and prepare for a more secure future. Estate planning typically relates to other complex, long-term goals and enables advisors to operate in a more holistic and meaningful way for their wealthy clients. Furthermore, life insurance is less dependent on investable or liquid assets and can often be creatively funded.

We believe the products and solutions in this book provide a unique opportunity for all types of advisors—but especially those that have not historically focused on estate planning or life insurance—to evolve their practices toward the wealth management model and expand their client relationships in preparation for better times ahead.

APPENDICES

APPENDIX A

■

HIGH-NET-WORTH
PSYCHOLOGY

It's common knowledge that segmentation allows you to understand more about your clients' specific attitudes and behaviors and connect more strongly with them. Fortunately, there are many ways that wealthy clients can be segmented; we find that by focusing on psychographic segments, rather than traditional demographic factors (such as gender or education level) we can uncover some distinct financial personalities within the affluent population.

Importantly, these personalities explain the overriding psychological motivation of a wealthy individual when it comes to their finances, their investment relationships and products, and their advisors. There are nine segments of high-net-worth investors (Exhibit A.1). These personalities are part of High-Net-Worth Psychology, a scientific process that can be a powerful tool for advisors who want to reach, connect, and cultivate wealthy clients over the long-term.

EXHIBIT A.1
High-Net-Worth Investor Segments

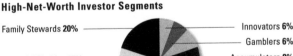

Family Stewards **20%** — Innovators **6%**
— Gamblers **6%**
Financial Phobics **17%** — Accumulators **8%**
Independents **13%** — VIPs **8%**
The Anonymous **12 %** — Moguls **10%**

EXHIBIT A.2
Segment Characteristics

Family Stewards	■ Focus on finances to take care of families ■ Are generally conservative ■ Not very knowledgeable about investing or the other disciplines that comprise financial planning
Financial Phobics	■ Avoid focusing on finances and related topics ■ Many have inherited their wealth ■ Often confused and frustrated by the responsibilities of wealth
Independents	■ Driven by the personal freedom that money makes possible ■ Believe planning and investing is a necessary means to an end ■ Not interested in the overarching process, just the results
Anonymous	■ Confidentiality is their primary concern ■ Demand privacy re: their financial affairs ■ Likely to concentrate their assets and have fewer advisory relationships than other personalities
Moguls	■ View financial management as another way of creating personal power ■ Control (or perceived control) is a primary concern ■ Highly decisive
VIPs	■ Investing success results in social recognition ■ Prestige is important ■ Want to work with "the best" institutions and advisors
Accumulators	■ Financial management is solely about making money ■ Are performance and results oriented ■ Are fairly knowledgeable and very involved
Gamblers	■ Relish the process of investing ■ Are very knowledgeable and heavily involved ■ Have a high risk tolerance and may make uninformed decisions
Innovators	■ Prefer leading-edge products and services ■ Are financially sophisticated and value complex products ■ Are technically savvy

The above table contains the key needs, values, and motivations for each of the nine personalities (Exhibit A.2).

Profile Your Clients

Knowing the psychological motivation of your clients is the first step toward a stronger and more effective connection with them. It will also allow you to establish a meaningful link between your services and their needs. Use these diagnostic questions to help you determine the psychological personalities of your wealthy clients and prospects.

1. What would you like your investments to achieve?

Follow-Up: Is it to take care of your family or to be more personally independent?

2. When you think about your money, what concerns, needs, or feeling come to mind?

Follow-Up: Are you more interested in accumulating money or what money can do for you?

3. How involved do you like to be in the investing process?

Follow-Up: Is investing something you *like* to do or *have* to do?

4. How important to you is the confidentiality of your financial affairs?

Follow-Up: Is there anyone else who needs to be included in our planning decisions?

APPENDIX B

■

THE IMPLEMENTATION
OF OBSTACLES
OF ESTATE PLANNING

Adapted from Square Peg, Round Hole *by Hannah Shaw Grove and Russ Alan Prince*
Private Wealth: Advising the Exceptionally Affluent, *August/September 2008*

Developing a comprehensive estate plan with an experienced legal professional can cost tens of thousands of dollars. Not having an estate plan in place and operational at the time of death can cost both time and money in the form of unnecessary complications and taxes for the estate's heirs. This is the reason many wealthy individuals decide to create estate plans in the first place; there is general agreement that having an estate plan can be a thoughtful and pragmatic step toward ensuring that the greatest amount of an estate's assets make it to the designated people and organizations. Unfortunately, many plans never become real, getting derailed before documents are drafted and executed and the trusts, partnerships, and other legal structures are created. We spoke separately to trusts and estates attorneys and affluent individuals to compare their views on the situation and understand why.

Nonchalant Professionals
In 2003, and again in 2006, we conducted separate surveys with trusts and estates attorneys who had designed and prepared estate plans for wealthy cli-

ents that had not been implemented. Given the amount of effort and expertise it takes to develop an estate plan, we were surprised to find almost no concern among these attorneys for their clients' lack of follow-through. In 2003, just 17% of them expressed concerned and the number dropped sharply to about 7% three years later (Exhibit B.1).

EXHIBIT B.1
Few Attorneys are Concerned by a Lack of Implementation

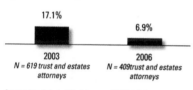

Source: The Private Client Lawyer *(2003)* & Prince and Associates, Inc. *(2006)*

Next we asked about the type of follow-up initiated by the attorneys to encourage plan implementation. Roughly 80% of attorneys that expressed concern about their clients' inaction sent letters or e-mails suggesting they come in to sign their documents. Very few—only 13% of them—initiated personal contact either by calling or arranging a meeting (Exhibit B.2). While those figures may seem grim, the lack of follow-up by unconcerned attorneys was startling. More than 80% of them matched their clients' lack of action with their own and did nothing to promote further activity. Just 17% sent letters and e-mails, and only 1% placed phone calls.

EXHIBIT B.2
Actions Taken to Promote Implemenation

ACTION	CONCERNED	NOT CONCERNED
No action	8.2%	82.2%
Sent a letter or email	78.4%	16.7%
Telephone contact	11.9%	1.1%
Meeting with the client	1.5%	0.0%
	N = 134 attorneys	*N = 1,027 attorneys*

Source: The Private Client Lawyer *(2003)* & Prince and Associates, Inc. *(2006)*

The reasons behind the attorneys' apathy lie in the very nature of the trusts and estates business. It is largely transactional, meaning that lawyers are retained to work on a specific project or plan. Estate plans are long-term initiatives—designed to work over a period of many years—so once a project or a plan has been completed the lawyers must find new clients. In effect, they close the books and move on without dwelling on whether their plan ever makes it to fruition. Furthermore, once a client has paid their bill, making sure the documents are signed becomes less important.

While this seems to be the status quo, it is an unsustainable situation for both trusts and estates attorneys and wealthy individuals that need estate planning expertise.

Dissatisfied Customers

To understand why many wealthy individuals choose not to follow through on their estate planning efforts, we constructed survey samples in 2003 and 2006 with families with net-worths in excess of $10 million that had done just that.

The overriding reason cited in both studies was that the estate plan did not satisfy their goals, wants, and objectives (Exhibit B.3). Many clients begin the process not knowing exactly what they want, or unable to express it clearly, hoping that the attorney will be able to guide them through the process and help them crystallize their priorities and values. In the case of abandoned estate plans, the attorneys were clearly unsuccessful in identifying their clients' core issues but proceeded with plan development anyway.

Furthermore, most families felt uncomfortable with the attorney they had retained which had a direct impact on their interest in pursuing the process. Unease is a typical reaction when service professionals are perceived as poor listeners, are not ap-

EXHIBIT B.3
The Decision Not to Implement

ISSUE	2003 STUDY	2006 STUDY
The estate plan did not deal with the affluent client's goals, wants, needs, and objectives	87.2%	95.9%
The trusts and estates lawyer made them uneasy	82.3%	93.4%
The estate plan was too complicated	53.1%	55.3%
	N = 288 wealthy families	N = 197 wealthy families

Source: The Private Client Lawyer *(2003)* & Prince and Associates, Inc. *(2006)*

propriately empathetic, function clinically, or are not consultative in their approach. Interestingly, and perhaps related, is that dissatisfaction among clients has escalated in the three years between studies while concern among attorneys has diminished.

It's worth noting that roughly half of families surveyed in both studies felt their estate plans were too complicated to implement. Ironically, most affluent families expect sophisticated and intricate strategies from their attorneys in order to protect their wealth. Nevertheless, it's clear that many trusts and estates lawyers fail to assess their clients' level of knowledge about estate planning and their comfort with complexity, and do a feeble job explaining abstract legal concepts to laypeople.

Confusing AND Condescending

Adding insult to injury, it seems that many trusts and estates attorneys have other weaknesses when it comes to client interaction. Most of the families surveyed said they were unable to determine if the final plan presented by their attorney was, in fact, going to help them accomplish their objectives (Exhibit B.4). Their attorneys did not, or could not, explain how the plan would work and their role in the process. Clients felt further alienated by the lawyers' overuse of legal jargon and condescending behavior. Further analysis revealed that the perception of arrogance was derived from consistent use of legal terminology, a "presumptuous air

EXHIBIT B.4
How Attorneys Fail to Communicate

STATEMENT	2003 STUDY	2006 STUDY
I couldn't tell if the plan did what I wanted it to do	80.6%	90.9%
My attorney didn't speak in "English"	70.1%	81.7%
Often used legal terms I didn't understand	65.6%	80.2%
My attorney talked "down" to me	31.6%	46.2%
	N = 288 wealthy families	N = 197 wealthy families

Source: The Private Client Lawyer (2003) & Prince and Associates, Inc. (2006)

of authority", and unwillingness to devote extra time to helping clients understand the details and nuances of their plan.

Across the board, trusts and estates attorneys were rated much lower by their clients in 2006 than they were just three years earlier, underscoring their inability to communicate the value of their work and the financial pressure facing attorneys with a largely transactional business model.

An Exercise in Futility

As noted previously, affluent clients have a lot at risk when they choose not to implement an estate plan. However, our research shows that trusts and estates attorneys have much at stake as well when they leave their clients unsatisfied.

We all recognize that one bad experience can have an insidious and lasting effect and, in this case, can cast a pall over both the attorney and the law firm. Very few of the wealthy clients surveyed expect to work with the lawyer or the firm again and a similarly low number would refer a family member, friend, or business associate to the firm (Exhibit B.5). What's worse is that instead of simply choosing to work with another attorney or directing their colleagues and confidants elsewhere, these unhappy and dissatisfied clients will advise other people to avoid the professional or the firm altogether.

EXHIBIT B.5
Future Actions

ACTION	2003 STUDY	2006 STUDY
Do more business with the attorney or the law firm	9.4%	4.6%
Refer other people to the attorney or the law firm	7.3%	3.6%
Recommend other people *avoid* the attorney or the law firm	69.1%	74.1%
	N = 288 wealthy families	N = 197 wealthy families

Source: The Private Client Lawyer *(2003)* & Prince and Associates, Inc. *(2006)*

These simple actions, while imperceptible to the trusts and estates attorney, can have a compounded effect and cause business to flatline or suffer. As with the other areas discussed, proportionately more clients are critical of their experience and their professionals in 2006 than they were in 2003. In that period of time, the structure of the trusts and estates business has become less client-oriented and, therefore, less client-friendly while the super-wealthy have become more astute and demanding purchasers of professional services.

APPENDIX C

■

THE IMPLICATIONS OF STATE DEATH TAXES

*Adapted from "The State Matters" by Richard P. Breed, III
and Jennifer A. Civitella of Tarlow, Breed, Hart & Rodgers, P.C.*
Private Wealth: Advising the Exceptionally Affluent, *April/May 2008*

As the federal estate tax exemption climbs, and as the 2010 repeal approaches, many families and their advisors are relieved that $2 million to $7 million of assets can be inherited federal estate tax-free. However, residents of most states must still plan for looming, and often substantial, state death taxes.

In 2000, most states imposed an estate tax to the extent of the state death tax credit under section 2011 of the Internal Revenue Code (the "Code"). Their estate tax systems were "coupled" with the Code and "picked-up" an estate tax to the extent of section 2011's credit allowance.

Until 2001, the typical estate plan of a married couple with a federal taxable estate provided for the estate of the first deceased spouse to be divided into two shares. One share (the "Credit Shelter Trust") would be funded with an amount equal to the applicable federal estate tax exemption. The balance of the deceased spouse's estate would fund the "Marital Deduction Trust" which qualified for the marital deduction, usually achieved by making a "QTIP election." As a result of this estate planning technique, both federal and state estate taxes would be deferred until the death of the surviving spouse.

Example 1

Married Maine resident (a "pick-up" state) died in 2000 with a gross estate of $3,000,000. Decedent's Revocable Trust provided for his estate to be divided into two shares: a Credit Shelter Trust equal to the applicable federal estate tax exemption at the time of his death ($675,000) and a Marital Deduction Trust equal to the balance of his estate ($2,325,000). This formula would result in no estate tax liability at the first spouse's death and would fully "fund" his federal estate tax exemption.

The Economic Growth and Tax Relief Reconciliation Act of 2001 ("EGTRRA") changed the federal estate tax system significantly: the applicable federal exemption was increased; the maximum federal estate tax rate was decreased; and the state death tax credit under section 2011 was gradually phased out and replaced with a deduction under section 2058 for state estate taxes paid.

The repeal of the credit pulled the rug out from under the "pick-up" states. They were left with two choices: do nothing, and allow the state's death tax to evaporate with the repeal of the section 2011 credit, or respond with legislation to "de-couple" from the federal estate tax system. About one-third of the "pick-up" states have eliminated their states' death tax. Several others have separated entirely from the federal estate tax system and have enacted their own independent inheritance or estate tax. The remaining "pick-up" states have "de-coupled" from the federal estate tax, but are "coupled" with a pre-EGTRRA version of the Code.

Most estate plans drafted prior to 2001 provide for maximum estate tax deferral based on a "coupled" state-federal estate tax system. Such estate plans may no longer provide the desired estate tax deferral because of the new state death tax laws.

Example 2

A married New Jersey resident dies in 2008 with a gross estate of $3,000,000. His Revocable Trust directs his estate to be divided into two shares: the Credit Shelter Trust would be funded with the applicable federal estate tax exemption ($2,000,000) and the Marital Deduction Trust would be funded with the balance of the estate ($1,000,000). New Jersey "de-coupled" in 2002 and limited its applicable exemption to $675,000. The estate tax liability would be $99,600.

Credit Shelter Trust Planning

A state death tax liability may be looming for older estate plans that have not been updated since EGTRRA. Estate plans of a married couple may be amended so upon the death of the first spouse, the decedent's estate is divided into three shares. The first share (the "Credit Shelter Trust") is equal to the applicable state estate tax exemption and will not be subject to any estate taxes. The second share (the "State QTIP Trust") is funded with an amount equal to the difference between the deceased spouse's state exemption and federal exemption and will be subject to the state's death tax upon surviving spouse's death. The third share (the "Federal QTIP Trust") is funded with the balance of the decedent's estate and will be subject to both federal and state estate taxes upon surviving spouse's death. Complete estate tax deferral is possible by making a state-only QTIP election to the State QTIP Trust, thereby qualifying it for the marital deduction for state estate tax purposes. Both federal and state QTIP elections will be made for the Federal QTIP Trust.

Example 3

A married Rhode Island resident dies in 2008 with a taxable estate of $3,000,000. Pursuant to his updated Revocable Trust, the decedent's estate would be divided into the following three shares: the Credit Shelter Trust would be funded with $675,000, an amount equal to the Rhode Island estate tax exemption, the Rhode Island QTIP Trust would be funded with $1,325,000, an amount equal to the difference between the applicable federal estate tax exemption ($2,000,000) and the Rhode Island exemption; and the Federal QTIP Trust would be funded with $1,000,000, the balance of Decedent's estate.

Some states permit estates to make a state-only QTIP election. However, not all states permit an independent state QTIP election to be made when a federal QTIP election has not been. For residents of these states, the decision must be made whether to pay state estate taxes at the first spouse's death or defer estate taxes until the surviving spouse's death. The drawback to complete deferral is the increase in the size of the surviving spouse's taxable estate for federal estate tax purposes.

Example 4

A married New York resident dies in 2009 with a taxable estate of $5,000,000. Pursuant to her pre-EGTRRA Revocable Trust, the decedent's estate would be divided into two shares: the Credit Shelter Trust would be funded with $3,500,000, an amount equal to the available federal estate tax exemption; and the Marital Deduction Trust would be funded with $1,500,000, the balance of her estate. Federal and New York QTIP elections would be made for the Marital Deduction Trust. Since New York has "de-coupled" and frozen its estate tax exemption at $1,000,000, the New York estate tax liability would be $229,200.

Example 5

Assume the same facts as above, except the decedent's estate plan has been amended since EGTRRA. The Credit Shelter Trust would be funded with an amount equal to the lesser of the federal estate tax exemption or the New York estate tax exemption at the time of the decedent's death, $1,000,000. The balance of the decedent's estate would fund the Marital Deduction Trust, $4,000,000. Federal and New York QTIP elections would be made for the Marital Deduction Trust. At the time of the decedent's death, the applicable federal estate tax exemption is $3,500,000. $2,500,000 of this exemption would be unused. Depending on the size of the surviving spouse's taxable estate when he dies, this may be up to an additional federal estate tax of $1,125,000, significantly higher than the estate tax liability at the first death in Example 4.

Planning for the Patchwork State Estate Tax

A significant state death tax liability may arise as a result of a decedent having assets in multiple states. The estate tax rules of many states assume that all states are based on the IRC section 2011 state death tax credit. For example, the Massachusetts estate tax applicable to its residents is based on the decedent's federal gross estate, i.e., all of decedent's property, no matter where located. The Massachusetts estate tax liability is decreased by death taxes paid to other jurisdictions. What if the decedent has property in a state in which there is no death tax?

Example 6

A widowed Massachusetts resident dies in 2008 with a $3,000,000 taxable estate consisting of a $1,000,000 Miami condominium and $2,000,000 Massachusetts property. Massachusetts "de-coupled" in July 2002 and froze its estate tax exemption at $1,000,000 beginning in 2006. Florida does not have a state death tax. For Massachusetts estate tax purposes, the Miami condominium is included in the decedent's gross estate. The Massachusetts estate tax would be $182,000, although the tax on the Massachusetts property would be $99,600.

Example 7

A widowed Florida resident dies in 2008 with a $3,000,000 taxable estate consisting of a $2,000,000 Boston condominium and $1,000,000 Florida property. The decedent does not own the condominium outright; she owns it as the sole member of a Limited Liability Company ("LLC"), used for holding title because it is rental property. The Massachusetts estate tax applicable to non-residents applies to Massachusetts real estate; it does not apply to intangible personal property, such as a membership interest in an LLC. There is no state death tax liability.

Advisors cannot assume that because a client does not have a federal taxable estate, state death taxes are not relevant, especially as states feel the "pinch" from the post-EGTRRA drop in revenue. A careful analysis is necessary to determine the proper plan to minimize, defer, or pay state death taxes. Such analysis should also consider both the applicable estate taxes of the client's domicile and the estate taxes of all states in which the client may own property.

APPENDIX D

■

ASSET PROTECTION

Adapted from *Fame & Fortune: Maximizing Celebrity Wealth*
by Russ Alan Prince, Hannah Shaw Grove & Richard J. Flynn, Universal Media,
2008 and *Fortune's Fortress: A Primer of Wealth Preservation for
Hedge Fund Professionals* by Russ Alan Prince, Edward A. Renn,
Arthur A. Bavelas and Mindy F. Rosenthal, MarHedge, 2007.

Asset protection is a component of advanced planning that helps the high-net-worth structure their wealth in ways that deter gold diggers, business creditors, disillusioned ex-spouses, jilted lovers, unhappy investors, and the like. Regrettably, many affluent individuals know from experience that facing a lawsuit without completing any asset protection planning can be costly and painful.

Asset protection can be accomplished in a number of ways but, like other components of advanced planning, it is unique to the owner of the asset and the surrounding circumstances. Asset protection must be approached as part of an overall financial plan and demonstrate that the strategies are morally and economically sound in order to pass legal inspection.

In an ideal world, everyone would be prepared for unexpected events and disasters. But you don't have to be a pessimist to plan for the worst. It's possible to manage risks in ways that will protect clients and their assets from unwanted attention and unfounded legal action. The key is to do it in a timely and effective fashion that has little to no downside—and that's the role that asset protection can play.

While asset protection is a discrete form of legal planning, it is a derivative of other disciplines such as risk management. The goal is to provide a client and his or her assets with a viable defense against litigants and creditors.

So, what is "asset protection?" Simply put:

Asset protection planning is the process of employing risk management products and legally acceptable strategies to ensure a person's wealth is not unjustly taken from him or her.

The preferred course of action—for most people—is to avoid litigation, especially from baseless claims. The best asset protection plans are never even tested in court; after reviewing the way assets have been structured, creditors and litigants conclude that going to court would be too costly and difficult, and they choose to settle. Those cases that do make it to trial often result in small or unpaid judgments, as the assets are simply and legitimately not accessible.

Critical to successful asset protection planning is timing. By and large, you have to implement strategies that would effectively protect wealth before the problems arise. In essence, it's a form of *pre-litigation* planning. While certain circumstances permit individuals to use asset protection strategies after the fact, they are relatively few and far between.

The Court's Perspective

Not surprisingly, judges and juries tend to frown on wealthy and successful people that try to avoid paying their debts. As such, the transactions and structures that protect the wealth (especially the wealth of high-profile individuals such as celebrities and hedge fund partners) from creditors should make economic sense within the context of an overall financial plan. This means that asset protection planning, to the extent possible, should happen in conjunction with or as an offshoot of other legal planning efforts. Not only is this a logical approach from a financial perspective, it provides a built-in rationale for each action should they come under scrutiny.

Solid asset protection planning must justify the way wealth is organized and the manner in which assets were transferred into various legal structures such as trusts, partnerships, and corporate entities. The advanced planner must be capable of presenting the facts surrounding the implementation of asset protection strategies in a way that will resonate with a judge or jury and demonstrate that:

■ The targeted individual was morally right in his or her actions.
■ The strategies implemented were economically and legally sound given the targeted individual's personal, professional, and financial situation.

Protecting Celebrity Wealth

Like most wealthy individuals, celebrities focus on protecting their assets only after they have had their fortunes risked or lost. Unfortunately, that is often too late. The time to prepare for unjust legal actions is before they occur.

EXHIBIT D.1
Been Involved in Unjust Lawsuits and/or Divorce Proceedings

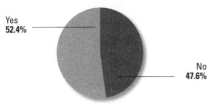

Yes
52.4%

No
47.6%

N = 1,015 celebrities (based on 203 entertainment attorneys)

The data presented in this section was collected with the assistance of entertainment attorneys from more than 1,000 celebrities. The average net worth of the individuals surveyed was $37 million and the median net worth was $25 million.

As it turns out, more than half of celebrities surveyed have already been involved in unjust lawsuits or divorce proceedings (Exhibit D.1). This figure is much higher than it is for the rest of the wealthy population, likely due to the high profile of celebrities and the warped public perception of celebrity wealth. It's frightening how quickly a lawsuit can materialize when people think you're amazingly wealthy.

Clearly, the bad memories have lingered as most celebrities are concerned about future involvement in similar cases. About 85% of celebs are anxious about being targeted further (Exhibit D.2). After all, an unfavorable legal decision or a messy divorce can decimate years of wealth creation. Most celebrities have an overwhelming, but often unvoiced, fear that a judge and jury will have a bias against them due to their wealth and assume they can easily afford losses.

EXHIBIT D.2
Concerned About Being Involved in Unjust Lawsuits and/or Divorce Proceedings

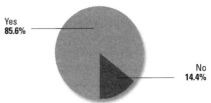

Yes
85.6%

No
14.4%

N = 1,015 celebrities (based on 203 entertainment attorneys)

We found that asset protection planning carries the same sense of urgency as its advanced planning counterparts—wealth enhancement and estate planning—for wealthy celebrities. Even though most celebs find the idea of a smaller tax bill appealing, very few had engaged in proper wealth enhancement activities. And a similarly large number of celebrities wanted to control the disposition of their estate, but very few had up-to-date estate plans. Sadly, there is very little difference when it comes to asset protection despite significant experience with unfounded lawsuits. Even though 86% of celebrities feared future law suits, only 28% had taken the steps to protect

EXHIBIT D.3
Have an Asset Protection Plan

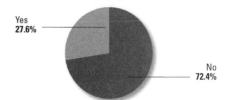

N = 1,015 celebrities (based on 203 entertainment attorneys)

their assets (Exhibit D.3).

As in our analysis of the celebs without a current estate plan, we used factor analysis to identify the principal motivation for not having an asset protection plan. By and large, the main reason most celebs didn't have plans was because no one with the expertise had introduced the topic and shown them how. A much smaller group cited complexity as a deterrent to asset protection and just a handful were unsure about the legality of such planning or felt they had no need to protect their wealth (Exhibit D.4).

EXHIBIT D.4
Why No Asset Protection Plan

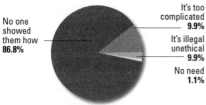

N = 1,015 celebrities (based on 203 entertainment attorneys)

Protecting Hedge Fund Wealth

Given the size of their personal fortunes and the incessant media coverage underscoring the lucrative fee structures of alternative investments, it's understandable that hedge fund professionals generally echo the sentiments of celebrities when it comes to asset protection.

The data presented in this section was collected from 294 executives at hedge fund or hedge fund-of-fund firms. The average net worth of the principals surveyed was $197 million and the median net worth was $62 million.

EXHIBIT D.5
Been Involved in Unjust Lawsuits and/or Divorce Proceedings

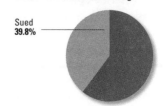

N = 294 hedge fund professionals

About 40% of the wealthy professionals we surveyed had been involved in unjust lawsuits or divorce proceedings (Exhibit D.5). We also found that most hedge fund executives understand the consequences of such situations as 83% of them are concerned about future involved in such cases (Exhibit D.6).

While the logic for establishing an asset protection plan is compelling, less than half of survey respondents had done so (Exhibit D.7) and many of those are out of date. Although hedge fund professionals are better prepared than celebrities are, there is still a significant gap between the level of concern and the action taken to prevent or manage such unwelcome scenarios.

EXHIBIT D.6
Concerned About Being Involved in Unjust Lawsuits and/or Divorce Proceedings

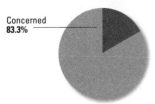

Concerned
83.3%

N = 294 hedge fund professionals

Implications for the Wealthy and Their Advisors

Protecting a fortune can be an important and emotional issue for many, especially for those who are under constant appraisal by opportunists. Most wealthy individuals are familiar with groundless claims and costly legal proceedings, but very few have taken the steps to prepare themselves for future onslaughts. Fortunately, this is a situation that can be easily corrected.

EXHIBIT D.7
Have an Asset Protection Plan

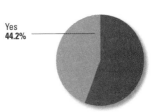

Yes
44.2%

N = 294 hedge fund professionals

Advisors must familiarize themselves with the techniques and structures that enable asset protection, how each can function as part of an overarching financial program, and the legal criteria that must be met in order to be deemed effective in a court of law. Finally, having a strong network of advanced planning specialists will allow for responsiveness and action when it is most needed.

ABOUT THE AUTHORS

Russ Alan Prince is the world's leading authority on private wealth, the author of more than 40 books on the topic, and a highly-sought counselor to families with significant global resources and their advisors.
www.russalanprince.com • russ@russalanprince.com

Hannah Shaw Grove is a widely recognized author, columnist and speaker, and an expert on the mindset, behaviors, concerns, preferences, and finances of high-net-worth individuals.
www.hsgrove.com • hannah@hsgrove.com

Brett Van Bortel is an authority on practice management and leads Van Kampen's Consulting Services HNW client acquisition and retention programs.
www.vankampen.com • brett.vanbortel@vankampen.com

Richard L. Harris, CLU, AEP, is managing member of BPN Montaigne LLC, a firm that specializes in advanced insurance planning for high-net-worth clients.
www.bpnmont.com • richard@bpnmont.com

ABOUT THE PUBLISHER

Charter Financial Publishing Network is a management-owned company led by some of the most experienced and respected publishing professionals in the industry including editor-in-chief Evan Simonoff, group publisher David Smith, and president and CEO Charlie Stroller. Their portfolio of business interests is diverse and includes magazines, newsletters, conferences, educational and e-commerce websites, and marketing databases. Their flagship publications—*Financial Advisor, Private Wealth* and *The Journal of Indexes*—deliver timely insights to more than 100,000 financial professionals each month.

www.fa-mag.com • www.pw-mag.com • www.indexuniverse.com